MATTHEW

Chapters 14—28

J. Vernon McGee

THOMAS NELSON PUBLISHERS

Nashville • Atlanta • London • Vancouver

Published in Nashville, Tennessee, by Thomas Nelson, Inc.

Scripture quotations are from the KING JAMES VERSION of the Bible.

Library of Congress Cataloging-in-Publication Data

McGee, J. Vernon (John Vernon), 1904–1988
   [Thru the Bible with J. Vernon McGee]
   Thru the Bible commentary series / J. Vernon McGee.
      p.   cm.
   Reprint. Originally published: Thru the Bible with J. Vernon
McGee. 1975.
   Includes bibliographical references.
   ISBN 0-7852-1038-5 (TR)
   ISBN 0-7852-1098-9 (NRM)
   1. Bible—Commentaries. I. Title.
BS491.2.M37   1991
220.7'7—dc20   90–41340
                                      CIP

PRINTED IN MEXICO
20 21 22 23 - 10 09 08

CONTENTS

MATTHEW—Chapters 14—28

PREFACE

The radio broadcasts of the Thru the Bible Radio five-year program were transcribed, edited, and published first in single-volume paperbacks to accommodate the radio audience.

There has been a minimal amount of further editing for this publication. Therefore, these messages are not the word-for-word recording of the taped messages which went out over the air. The changes were necessary to accommodate a reading audience rather than a listening audience.

These are popular messages, prepared originally for a radio audience. They should not be considered a commentary on the entire Bible in any sense of that term. These messages are devoid of any attempt to present a theological or technical commentary on the Bible. Behind these messages is a great deal of research and study in order to interpret the Bible from a popular rather than from a scholarly (and too-often boring) viewpoint.

We have definitely and deliberately attempted "to put the cookies on the bottom shelf so that the kiddies could get them."

The fact that these messages have been translated into many languages for radio broadcasting and have been received with enthusiasm reveals the need for a simple teaching of the whole Bible for the masses of the world.

I am indebted to many people and to many sources for bringing this volume into existence. I should express my especial thanks to my secretary, Gertrude Cutler, who supervised the editorial work; to Dr. Elliott R. Cole, my associate, who handled all the detailed work with the publishers; and finally, to my wife Ruth for tenaciously encouraging me from the beginning to put my notes and messages into printed form.

Solomon wrote, ". . . of making many books there is no end; and much study is a weariness of the flesh" (Eccl. 12:12). On a sea of books that flood the marketplace, we launch this series of THRU THE BIBLE with the hope that it might draw many to the one Book, *The Bible.*

J. Vernon McGee

The Gospel According to

MATTHEW

INTRODUCTION

The Gospel of Matthew, although it is only twenty-eight chapters long, is a very important book. In fact, Genesis and Matthew are the two key books of the Bible.

As we come today to the Gospel of Matthew, I'd like to bridge the gap between the Old Testament and the New Testament because, in order to appreciate and to have a right understanding of the New Testament, it is almost essential to know something about this period of approximately four hundred years. This is the time span between the days of Nehemiah and Malachi and the birth of Jesus Christ in Bethlehem. You see, after Malachi had spoken, heaven went silent. Station G O D went off the air, and there was no broadcasting for four hundred years. Then one day the angel of the Lord broke in upon the time of prayer when there was a priest by the name of Zacharias standing at the altar in Jerusalem. The angel gave the announcement of the birth of John the Baptist who was the forerunner of the Lord Jesus. We shall see later how important John the Baptist is in the Gospel of Matthew.

We find that a great deal took place in this interval of four hundred years even though it is a silent period as far as Scripture is concerned. This period was a thrilling and exciting time in the history of these people, and in many ways it was also a tragic time. The internal condition of Judah experienced a radical transformation. A new culture, different institutions, and unfamiliar organizations arose in this period, and many of these new things appear in the New Testament.

World history had made tremendous strides in the interval between the Old and New Testaments. The Old Testament closed with the Medo-Persian Empire being the dominant power. Also, Egypt was still a power to be reckoned with in world politics. During the interval between the testaments, both faded from the scene as outstanding nations. World power shifted from the East to the West, from the Orient to the Occident, from Asia to Europe, and from Medo-Persia to Greece. When the New Testament opens, a new power, Rome, is the world ruler. A consideration of some important dates will give a bird's-eye view of this great transition period. (Because historians differ in their dating, consider these dates as approximate.)

480 B.C. Xerxes, the Persian, was victorious against the Greeks at Thermopylae but was defeated at the battle of Salamis. Actually, it was a storm that defeated him. This was the last bid of the East for world dominion.

333 B.C. Out of the West there came that "goat" which Daniel records in the eighth chapter of Daniel. This was Alexander the Great, the goat with the great horn. He led the united Greek forces to victory over the Persians at Issus.

332 B.C. Alexander the Great visited Jerusalem. He was shown the prophecy of Daniel which spoke of him; therefore he spared Jerusalem. Jerusalem was one of the few cities that he ever spared.

323 B.C. Alexander died way over in Persia. Apparently he had intended to move the seat of his empire there. Then the world empire of both East and West was divided among his four generals.

320 B.C. Judea was annexed to Egypt by Ptolemy Soter.

312 B.C. Seleucus founded the kingdom of the Seleucidae, which is Syria. He attempted to take Judea, and so Judea became the battleground between Syria and Egypt. This little country became a buffer state.

203 B.C. Antiochus the Great took Jerusalem, and Judea passed under the influence of Syria.

170 B.C. Antiochus Epiphanes took Jerusalem and defiled the temple. He had been mentioned in Daniel as the "little

horn" (Dan. 8:9). He has been called the "Nero of Jewish history."

166 B.C. Mattathias, the priest of Judea, raised a revolt against Syria. This is the beginning of the Maccabean period. Probably the nation of Israel has never suffered more than during this era, and they were never more heroic than during this interval. Judas Maccabaeus, whose name means "the hammer," was the leader who organized the revolt.

63 B.C. Pompey, the Roman, took Jerusalem, and the people of Israel passed under the rulership of a new world power. They were under Roman government at the time of the birth of Jesus and throughout the period of the New Testament.

40 B.C. The Roman senate appointed Herod to be king of Judea. There never has been a family or a man more wicked than this. One can talk about the terrible Mafia, but this family would exceed them all.

37 B.C. Herod took Jerusalem and slew Antigonus the last of the Maccabean king-priests.

31 B.C. Caesar Augustus became emperor of Rome

19 B.C. The construction of the Herodian temple was begun. The building had been going on quite awhile when our Lord was born and was still continuing during the time of the New Testament.

4 B.C. Our Lord Jesus was born in Bethlehem.

Radical changes took place in the internal life of the nation of Judea because of their experiences during the intertestamental period. After the Babylonian captivity, they turned from idolatry to a frantic striving for legal holiness. The Law became an idol to them. The classic Hebrew gave way to the Aramaic in their everyday speech, although the Hebrew was retained for their synagogues. The synagogue seems to have come into existence after the Captivity. It became the center of their life in Judea and everywhere else they went in the world. Also, there arose among these people a group of parties which are mentioned in the New Testament and are never even heard of in the Old Testament:

1. *PHARISEES*—The Pharisees were the dominant party. They arose to defend the Jewish way of life against all foreign influences. They were strict legalists who believed in the Old Testament. They were nationalists in politics and wanted to restore the kingdom to the line of David. So they were a religio-political party. Today we would call them fundamental theologically and to the far right politically.

2. *SADDUCEES*—The Sadducees were made up of the wealthy and socially-minded who wanted to get rid of tradition. By the way, does that remind you of the present hour? Isn't it interesting that the rich families of this country are liberal? The crumbs still fall from the rich man's table. They are willing to give the crumbs, but they don't give their wealth, that is sure. The Sadducees were liberal in their theology, and they rejected the supernatural. Thus they were opposed to the Pharisees. The Sadducees were closely akin to the Greek Epicureans whose philosophy was "eat, drink, and be merry, for tomorrow we die." We may have a mistaken idea of the Sadducees. Actually, they were attempting to attain the "good life." They thought that they could overcome their bodily appetites by satisfying them, that by giving them unbridled reign, they would no longer need attention. In our day, a great many folk have this same philosophy. It did not work in the past; neither will it work today.

3. *SCRIBES*—The scribes were a group of professional expounders of the Law, stemming back from the days of Ezra. They became the hair-splitters. They were more concerned with the *letter* of the Law than with the *spirit* of the Law. When old Herod called in the scribes and asked where Jesus was to be born, they knew it was to be in Bethlehem. You would think that they would have hitchhiked a ride on the back of the camels to go down to Bethlehem to see Him, but they weren't interested. They were absorbed in the letter of the Law.

My friend, there is a danger of just wanting the information and the knowledge from the Bible but failing to translate it into shoe leather, not letting it become part of our lives. Through study we can learn the basic facts of Scripture, and all the theological truth contained in it, without allowing the Word of God to take possession of our hearts. The scribes fell into such a category. In our own day, I must confess that some of the most hard-hearted people I meet are fundamentalists. They are willing to rip a person apart in order to maintain some little point. It is important to know the Word of God—that is a laudable attainment—but also we are to translate it into life and pass it on to others.

4. *HERODIANS*—The Herodians were a party in the days of Jesus, and they were strictly political opportunists. They sought to maintain the Herods on the throne because they wanted their party in power.

The intertestamental period was a time of great literary activity in spite of the fact there was no revelation from God. The Old Testament was translated into Greek in Alexandria, Egypt, during the period from 285 to 247 B.C. It was translated by six members from each of the twelve tribes; hence, the name given to this translation was *Septuagint*, meaning "seventy." This translation was used by Paul, and our Lord apparently quoted from it.

The Apocrypha of the Old Testament was written in this era. These are fourteen books which bear no marks of inspiration. There are two books classified as the Pseudepigrapha, *Psalter of Solomon* and the *Book of Enoch*. They bear the names of two characters of the Old Testament, but there is no evidence that these two men were the writers.

Although this was a period marked by the silence of God, it is evident that God was preparing the world for the coming of Christ. The Jewish people, the Greek civilization, the Roman Empire, and the seething multitudes of the Orient were all being prepared for the coming of a Savior, insomuch that they produced the scene which Paul labeled, in Galatians 4:4, "the fulness of time." The four Gospels are directed to the four major groups in the world of that day.

The Gospel of Matthew was written to the nation Israel. It was first written in Hebrew, and it was directed primarily to the religious man of that time.

The Gospel of Mark was directed to the Roman. The Roman was a man of action who believed that government, law, and order could control the world. A great many people feel that is the way it should be done today. It is true that there must be law and order, but the Romans soon learned that they couldn't rule the world with that alone.

The world needed to hear about One who believed in law and order but who also offered the forgiveness of sins and the grace and the mercy of God. This is the Lord whom the Gospel of Mark presents to the Romans.

The Gospel of Luke was written to the Greek, to the thinking man.

The Gospel of John was written directly for believers but indirectly for the Orient where there were the mysterious millions, all crying out in that day for a deliverance.

There is still a crying out today from a world that needs a Deliverer. The religious man needs Christ and not religion. The man of power needs a Savior who has the power to save him. The thinking man needs One who can meet all his mental and spiritual needs. And certainly the wretched man needs to know about a Savior who not only can save him but build him up so that he can live for God.

The Gospel of Matthew was written by a publican whom the Lord Jesus had put His hand upon in a very definite way (see Matt. 9:9). He was a follower, a disciple, of the Lord Jesus. Papias says, Eusebius confirms, and other of the apostolic fathers agree, that this Gospel was written originally by Matthew in Hebrew for the nation Israel, a religious people.

I don't have time to give the background of all this, but God has prepared this whole nation for the coming of Christ into the world. And He did come of this nation, as the Lord Jesus Himself said, ". . . salvation is of the Jews" (John 4:22). It was a great German historian who said that God prepared the Savior to come out of Israel— "salvation is of the Jews"—and He prepared the heathen for salvation because they were lost and needed it.

This remarkable book is a key book of the Bible because it swings back into the Old Testament and gathers up more Old Testament prophecies than any other book. One might expect it to do this since it was first written to the Jews. But then, it moves farther into the New Testament than any of the other Gospels. For instance, no other Gospel writer mentions the church by name; but Matthew does. He is the one who relates the Word of our Lord, ". . . upon this rock I will build my church . . ." (Matt. 16:18). Even Renan, the French skeptic, said of this Gospel that it "is the most important book in Christendom, the most important that has ever been written." That is a remarkable statement coming from *him!* Matthew, a converted publican, was the choice of the Spirit of God to write this Gospel primarily to the people of Israel.

The Gospel of Matthew presents the program of God. The "kingdom of heaven" is an expression which is peculiar to this Gospel. It occurs thirty-two times. The word *kingdom* occurs fifty times. A proper understanding of the phrase "kingdom of heaven" is essential to any interpretation of this Gospel and of the Bible. May I make this statement right now, and I do make it categorically and dogmatically: The *Kingdom* and the *church* are not the same. They are not synonymous terms. Although the church is in the Kingdom, there is all the difference in the world.

For instance, Los Angeles is in California, but Los Angeles is not California. If you disagree, ask the people from San Francisco. California is not the United States, but it is in the United States. The Chamber of Commerce may think it is the United States, but it's not. It's only one-fiftieth of it.

Likewise, the church is in the Kingdom, but the Kingdom of Heaven, simply stated, is the reign of the heavens over the earth. The church is in this Kingdom. Now I know that theologians have really clouded the atmosphere, and they certainly have made this a very complicated thing. Poor preachers like I am must come up with a simple explanation, and this is it: the Kingdom of Heaven is the reign of the heavens over the earth. The Jews to whom this Gospel was directed understood the term to be the sum total of all the prophecies of the Old Testament concerning the coming of a King from heaven to set up a kingdom on this earth with heaven's standard. This term was not new to them (see Dan. 2:44; 7:14, 27).

The Kingdom of Heaven is the theme of this Gospel. The One who is going to establish that Kingdom on the earth is the Lord Jesus. The Kingdom is all important. The Gospel of Matthew contains three major discourses concerning the Kingdom.

1. *The Sermon on the Mount.* That is the *law* of the Kingdom. I think it is only a partial list of what will be enforced in that day.

2. *The Mystery Parables.* These parables in Matthew 13 are about

the Kingdom. Our Lord tells us that the Kingdom of Heaven is like a sower, like a mustard seed, and so on.

3. *The Olivet Discourse.* This looks forward to the establishment of the Kingdom here upon this earth.

It will be seen that the term "kingdom of heaven" is a progressive term in the Gospel of Matthew. This is very important for us to see. There is a movement in the Gospel of Matthew, and if we miss it, we've missed the gospel. It is like missing a turn-off on the freeway. You miss it, brother, and you're in trouble. So if we miss the movement in this marvelous Gospel, we miss something very important.

This Gospel is very much like the Book of Genesis. They are two key books of the Bible, and you really should be familiar enough with these two books so that you can *think* your way through them. I will be giving you chapter headings so you can learn to think your way through the book. I would tell my students in former days, "When you can't sleep at night, don't count sheep. Instead, think your way through Genesis. Then think your way through the Gospel of Matthew. Take it up chapter by chapter. Chapter One: what is it about? Chapter Two: what is it about? If you say to me that you don't like counting sheep or chapters, then talk to the Shepherd, but the finest way to talk to the Shepherd is to go through these two books. That will help you to get acquainted with Him and come to know Him." By the way, it's more important to have Him talk to us than for us to talk to Him. I don't know that I've got too much to tell Him, but He has a lot to tell me. I suggest that you learn the chapters of Matthew so that you don't miss the movement in them.

Now I want to give you one way of dividing the Gospel of Matthew. I'll follow a little different division, but this will help you to think it through. It is important to know Matthew in order to understand the Bible!

1. **Person** of the King
   Chapters 1—2
2. **Preparation** of the King
   Chapters 2—4:16

OUTLINE

CHAPTERS

CHAPTER 14

THEME: The forerunner, John the Baptist, is beheaded; Jesus withdraws but is followed by the multitude; He feeds the five thousand and sends His disciples over the sea into a storm, then walks on the water to them

The movement in Matthew of the rejection of Jesus as King and His conflict with the religious rulers continues. This chapter reveals that events are moving to a crisis. John the Baptist is slain on the pretext that Herod must keep his oath. This is an overt act of antagonism toward light and right which must ultimately lay wicked hands on Jesus. Jesus withdraws in order not to force the wicked hand of Herod, for the hour of Jesus has not yet come.

The feeding of the five thousand is certainly the most important of the miracles of Jesus if we are to judge by the attention given to it by the Gospel writers. It is the only miracle recorded by all the Gospel writers.

THE MURDER OF JOHN THE BAPTIST

At that time Herod the tetrarch heard of the fame of Jesus,

And said unto his servants, This is John the Baptist; he is risen from the dead; and therefore mighty works do shew forth themselves in him [Matt. 14:1–2].

If this sounds superstitious to you, you are right. It is superstitious, but it is not the superstition of the Bible nor of Jesus nor of His apostles, nor is it the superstition of Christianity. It is the superstition of old Herod and also of other ignorant people of that day. Somebody says, "Well, of course, in our contemporary society we are not superstitious like that." Aren't we? Notice how many people are following the horoscope and astrology charts. Also, religions of the Orient are having a tremendous influence in our modern culture. The human race is basically superstitious, my friend, and the minute you get away from the Word of God, you become superstitious. Even those who call themselves atheistic are turning to cults and "isms" and pagan religions, and we marvel that intelligent people could become involved in them.

The Person and the ministry of Jesus could not escape the notice of the king on the throne. Herod was a member of the family that you ought to look up in a good Bible dictionary. The whole family was a bunch of rascals and of the very darkest hue. They were the Mafia of the first century, and the Herod of this chapter was no exception.

The first several verses of this chapter are a flashback of what had already taken place. When Herod heard about the preaching of Jesus, he was immediately filled with fear and superstition. Herod had put John the Baptist to death, and he associated John with the Lord Jesus. Herod believed John had risen from the dead, and his fear changed to frenzy because he wanted to eliminate John altogether. Herod was a drunken, depraved, debased, weak man, and he was a killer. He had already murdered John, the forerunner of Christ, and he was prepared to murder the Lord Jesus Himself.

The following verses are part of the flashback describing the circumstances surrounding the death of John the Baptist.

For Herod had laid hold on John, and bound him, and put him in prison for Herodias' sake, his brother Philip's wife [Matt. 14:3].

Notice that it says that Herod *had* laid hold on John—it was a past action. Herod had imprisoned John "for Herodias' sake." Notice how Herod was influenced by others. Here it is by Herodias, and later on it will be by others. He was motivated like a politician. Everything he *did* was to gain the approval of others.

For John said unto him, It is not lawful for thee to have her [Matt. 14:4]

John the Baptist had spoken out against Herod's immorality—John wasn't a very good politician!

And when he would have put him to death, he feared the multitude, because they counted him as a prophet [Matt. 14:5].

Here we see that Herod was afraid of the crowd.

But when Herod's birthday was kept, the daughter of Herodias danced before them, and pleased Herod [Matt. 14:6].

Herod was a lascivious, lustful old creature, living with his brother's wife at the time, and John the Baptist had condemned him.

Whereupon he promised with an oath to give her whatsoever she would ask [Matt. 14:7].

He expected her to ask for some material thing, I suppose, and certainly something within reason.

And she, being before instructed of her mother, said, Give me here John Baptist's head in a charger [Matt. 14:8].

The mother, Herodias, lived up to the Herod name. Hers was a cruel and sadistic request, prompted by a brutal desire for revenge because of John's condemnation of her.

And the king was sorry: nevertheless for the oath's sake, and them which sat with him at meat, he commanded it to be given her [Matt. 14:9].

Imagine a man being motivated like that! He was afraid of what his guests might think of him for having made a promise and not making it good.

And he sent, and beheaded John in the prison.

And his head was brought in a charger, and given to the damsel: and she brought it to her mother [Matt. 14:10–11].

The sadistic, sad, and sordid account of what took place in that day reveals the type of society that existed then. John the Baptist was beheaded, and his head was given to the dancing girl on a platter! Human nature has not changed much. Lust and murder are part of contemporary society today.

And his disciples came, and took up the body, and buried it, and went and told Jesus [Matt. 14:12].

The disciples of John claimed his body and tenderly and lovingly buried it.

JESUS WITHDRAWS

The Lord withdrew because He knew that Herod's fear would break out into a frenzy and cause him to do something rash. The Lord Jesus knew this man and wanted to avoid an incident because His hour had not yet come.

When Jesus heard of it, he departed thence by ship into a desert place apart: and when the people had heard thereof, they followed him on foot out of the cities [Matt. 14:13].

The Lord went by ship across the Sea of Galilee, but the crowd that had followed Him on foot out of the cities did not want Him to leave, so they walked around the shore of Galilee and met Him on the other side. This reveals how popular He was with the crowds

> And Jesus went forth, and saw a great multitude, and was moved with compassion toward them, and he healed their sick [Matt. 14:14].

Notice again that they brought their sick folk out to Him. He healed literally thousands of people in that day. To compare what He did to the healing cults of our day is blasphemous. It casts a reflection on Him—because what He did was aboveboard and evident to everybody.

JESUS FEEDS THE HUNGRY

> And when it was evening, his disciples came to him, saying, This is a desert place, and the time is now past; send the multitude away, that they may go into the villages, and buy themselves victuals [Matt. 14:15].

Note that the disciples are attempting to advise Jesus what to do. Their advice was to send the people into the villages.

> But Jesus said unto them, They need not depart; give ye them to eat [Matt. 14:16].

The feeding of the five thousand is the one miracle which is recorded in all four Gospels. For that reason alone it is an important miracle.

It was as if the disciples had appointed themselves to the board of directors to tell the Lord Jesus what to do. But He said to them, "They need not depart; give ye them to eat." It was an impossible command.

> And they say unto him, We have here but five loaves, and two fishes [Matt. 14:17].

Having only five loaves and two fishes is typical of the sad state of the church in our day. Right now folk are saying that we need to send the multitudes away, that there are natural ways of caring for their needs. We send them to the psychiatrist for emotional help and to the government for physical relief. We do have spiritual bread to offer folk, although it may be only five loaves and two fishes, but the thing which is lacking is the power of the Lord Jesus. If we only had that power, we wouldn't need to send the multitudes away. We fail to realize that the solutions today are not in government nor in human imaginations but in God. No wonder the church is powerless.

He said, Bring them hither to me [Matt. 14:18].

I love that response! He is the Lord, my friend, and He says to us, "Bring what you have to Me." It is not what we have that counts with Him but actually what we don't have. The question is: Are we willing to release whatever we do have and let Him be the One to direct us in the disposition of it?

Don't get the impression that this little boy had five great big loaves of bread. They actually were little buns. There were over five thousand hungry people out there, and they had five little buns. This little boy had brought them—they were probably his lunch, and he could have eaten every bit of it. Five loaves and two small fish—and Jesus said, "Bring them hither to me."

And he commanded the multitude to sit down on the grass, and took the five loaves, and the two fishes, and looking up to heaven, he blessed, and brake, and gave the loaves to his disciples, and the disciples to the multitude [Matt. 14:19].

"He commanded the multitude to sit down on the grass." Someone has called our attention to something interesting here which most of us would have passed by. In Mark's account we are told that He made them sit down by companies or ranks, by hundreds and by fifties. These folk wore colorful clothing, and out there on the green grass they were seated probably by villages with each having its own distinct manner of dress. It must have been a thrilling sight to have seen this colorful group from the opposite hillside. They were probably wearing red, brown, blue, orange, and purple—probably a great deal of purple because purple dye was made in this area. It must have looked like one of those old-fashioned quilts. The Lord had them sit in order. The Lord did things orderly.

"And looking up to heaven, he blessed, and brake, and gave the loaves to his disciples, and the disciples to the multitude." These fellows who had appointed themselves to the board of directors in telling the Lord Jesus what to do find themselves now as waiters, serving the crowd. And that is really to be the particular ministry of apostles, disciples, ministers, evangelists, and all Christians in our day. We are to *feed* the multitude. There are too many people in our churches who want to tell how it should be done and too few who are willing to *do* it. A preacher said to me, "In my church we have all chiefs and no Indians. Everybody wants to be the head of something, chairman of a committee, or in another place of leadership." What the church needs is waiters to give out the Bread of Life, and the Bread is the Word of God. That's our business. All believers should be waiters passing it out.

> **And they did all eat, and were filled: and they took up of the fragments that remained twelve baskets full [Matt. 14:20].**

I formerly thought that taking up the "fragments" meant that they picked up what we would call the garbage; that is, someone bit into a sandwich, then put it down when he saw a bigger one, and the half-eaten sandwich would be a fragment. However, I realize now that here were twelve baskets of bread and fish which were never touched. It is difficult for us who live in the midst of supermarkets to understand that many of the world's population went to bed hungry last night. Most people in that day never knew what it was to have a full meal, but twelve baskets of food left over indicates that everyone had a full tummy.

> **And they that had eaten were about five thousand men, beside women and children [Matt. 14:21].**

There were five thousand men. This did not include the women and children. Is it too much to add one woman and one child to each man?

The Lord actually fed closer to fifteen thousand than to five thousand people that day.

JESUS WALKS ON THE WATER

As soon as the multitude was fed, Jesus sent his disciples to the other side of the Sea of Galilee, and He went to pray.

> **And straightway Jesus constrained his disciples to get into a ship, and to go before him unto the other side, while he sent the multitudes away [Matt. 14:22].**

"Straightway" is a word of urgency and swift movement. Matthew's record has a strange omission at the conclusion of the miracle of feeding the five thousand. He notes the urgency with which Jesus dismissed the multitudes and the haste in which He sent His disciples over the sea in the boat; however, he does not offer an explanation. John gives us the reason: "When Jesus therefore perceived that they would come and take him by force, to make him a king, he departed again into a mountain himself alone" (John 6:15). In view of the fact that Matthew is presenting that phase of the ministry of Jesus which has to do with His kingship, it may appear odd at first that he would ignore this attempt to make Jesus king. This is another evidence of the remarkable character of the claim of Jesus to be King. He is King by right and title. He will not become King by any democratic process. He is not "elected" King by the will of the people. He is King by the will of God. He will finally become King by force (see Ps. 2:8–9).

> **And when he had sent the multitudes away, he went up into a mountain apart to pray: and when the evening was come, he was there alone.**
>
> **But the ship was now in the midst of the sea, tossed with waves: for the wind was contrary [Matt. 14:23–24].**

The Lord is in the mountains, in the place of prayer. The disciples are down on the Sea of Galilee in a storm and in darkness; they are in the place of peril. What a picture this is of our own day. Our Lord has gone on to the Father and is seated at the Father's right hand. We today are down here on a storm-tossed sea in the place of peril.

I love this next verse—

> **And in the fourth watch of the night Jesus went unto them, walking on the sea [Matt. 14:25].**

The fourth watch is the morning watch, from three in the morning until daylight. This is the time the Lord walked on the sea, going to His disciples. And I think that will be the watch in which He will come for us at the Rapture. Christ is the bright and morning star for the church, and He will take the church out of the world. We don't know the date of His coming. There are men who would have us believe that they know the time, but they don't know. However, I believe that we are in the fourth watch of the night.

> **And when the disciples saw him walking on the sea, they were troubled, saying, It is a spirit; and they cried out for fear [Matt. 14:26].**

This is the picture: Our Lord is up there on the mountain, and He sees the disciples in the storm, toiling and rowing, as Mark's record has it. Then He comes to them in the fourth watch. When they see Him, they say, "It is a spirit; and they cried out for fear." Somebody is going to say, "Well, they were superstitious." Yes, there may have been a certain amount of superstition in them, but what would you think if a man came to you walking on the water? Many years ago over in Tennessee a fellow said, "l didn't believe in ghosts either until I saw one!" And that is the position of the disciples. They had never seen a spirit before, but they think they are seeing one now!

> **But straightway Jesus spake unto them, saying, Be of good cheer; it is I; be not afraid [Matt. 14:27].**

"Straightway Jesus spake unto them"—that is, *immediately* He reassured them that He was no ghost!

And Peter answered him and said, Lord, if it be thou, bid me come unto thee on the water [Matt. 14:28].

Peter has certainly been criticized for this. They say that he should not have asked to walk on water. Well, I rather admire the man. William Carey said, "Expect great things of God, and attempt great things for God." Certainly Peter did that! I am afraid that most of us are satisfied with little things from God.

Notice that Jesus did not rebuke Peter for asking—

And he said, Come. And when Peter was come down out of the ship, he walked on the water, to go to Jesus [Matt. 14:29].

I hear people say that Peter failed to walk on the water, but that is not the way my Bible reads. My Bible says that Peter *walked* on the water to go to Jesus. This is not failure! Peter asked a tremendous thing of God. No wonder God used him in such a wonderful way during the days that followed. No wonder he was chosen to preach the sermon on the Day of Pentecost.

But when he saw the wind boisterous, he was afraid; and beginning to sink, he cried, saying, Lord, save me [Matt. 14:30].

Peter took his eyes off the Lord Jesus while he was walking on the water. When he began to sink, he prayed the shortest prayer in the Bible, "Lord, save me"! If Simon Peter had prayed this prayer like some of us preachers pray, "Lord, Thou who are omnipotent, omniscient, omnipresent . . . ," Peter would have been twenty-nine feet under water before he would have gotten to his request. Peter got right down to business, and you and I need to pray like that.

And immediately Jesus stretched forth his hand, and caught him, and said unto him, O thou of little faith, wherefore didst thou doubt? [Matt. 14:31].

Peter's problem was that he took his eyes off Jesus and looked at the waves rolling. You and I are in a world today where we see the waves rolling, and this is the time when we need to keep our eyes on the Lord Jesus Christ.

And when they were come into the ship, the wind ceased.

Then they that were in the ship came and worshipped him, saying, Of a truth thou art the Son of God [Matt. 14:32–33].

Our Lord performed this miracle for His own, that they might be brought into the place of faith. Even Simon Peter, who was audacious enough to say, "Lord, bid me come unto thee on the water" and actually walked on the water, which should have cemented his faith, got his eyes off Jesus, and his faith failed. I don't want to criticize Peter because that has been my problem, also. I have stepped out on faith many times and then have taken my eyes off Him. This is the tragedy of the hour for us in our day. But these things were done that the disciples might worship Him and *know* that He was the Son of God.

And when they were gone over, they came into the land of Gennesaret.

And when the men of that place had knowledge of him, they sent out into all that country round about, and brought unto him all that were diseased;

And besought him that they might only touch the hem of his garment: and as many as touched were made perfectly whole [Matt. 14:34–36].

After the storm He continued to minister to the needs of the people. Again, let me call your attention to the multitudes that were healed in that day. We have a detailed record of only a few healings, but thousands were made whole by the Lord.

CHAPTER 15

THEME: Jesus denounces scribes and Pharisees; rebukes His disciples; heals the daughter of the
Syrophoenician woman and multitudes; feeds the
four thousand

This chapter continues the movement of the King, and He is beginning now to move toward the Cross. We have already seen His
rejection and conflict with the religious rulers. This chapter advances
the ministry of Jesus to the very breaking point with the scribes and
Pharisees. There is a lot of action here.

JESUS DENOUNCES THE SCRIBES AND PHARISEES

**Then came to Jesus scribes and Pharisees, which were
of Jerusalem, saying,**

**Why do thy disciples transgress the tradition of the el-
ders? for they wash not their hands when they eat bread
[Matt. 15:1–2].**

The scribes and the Pharisees had come all the way from Jerusalem.
In the previous chapter we saw that Jesus and His disciples were way
out in a desert place where the crowds couldn't even get to a ham-
burger stand; so He had fed them. On the surface it may seem like a
wonderful thing that the religious rulers had come all the way out to
listen to Him. Well, frankly, they hadn't come all the way out to ap-
plaud Him or to accept His teaching; they had come to criticize Him.
Immediately we recognize that this was not a friendly visit. They did
not accuse Him of breaking the Scriptures but of violating the tradi-
tions which they considered to be on a par with the Scriptures. They
wanted to know why His disciples did not wash their hands. They
were referring to a ceremonial cleansing rather than to what we would
consider a physical or sanitary washing. There are a great many peo-

ple who feel that if you go through some sort of an outward ceremony and clean up on the outside, this is all that is necessary.

> **But he answered and said unto them, Why do ye also transgress the commandment of God by your tradition? [Matt. 15:3].**

Jesus accuses them of breaking the commandment of God with their tradition. Their tradition, you see, permitted a man to disobey the Law, an amazing thing—and they had a very clever way of doing it.

> **For God commanded, saying, Honour thy father and mother: and, He that curseth father or mother, let him die the death.**

> **But ye say, Whosoever shall say to his father or his mother, It is a gift, by whatsoever thou mightest be profited by me;**

> **And honour not his father or his mother, he shall be free. Thus have ye made the commandment of God of none effect by your tradition [Matt. 15:4–6].**

Our Lord is saying that honoring father and mother includes supporting them. The way they got around that responsibility was to dedicate their money as a gift to God, and that would relieve them of supporting their parents. This gave a pious way out for a man to break the Mosaic Law.

I still believe the best way to test a Christian is by his pocketbook. The barometer of the Christian today is how he handles his own money and how he handles God's money. The religious rulers of Jesus' day were helping men escape their responsibility.

I am of the opinion that God wants you to pay your honest debts before you give to Him. God wants you to take care of your personal responsibilities. He wants you to support your family before you give to Him. I once knew a man with a wild idea. This man came to me on payday and wanted to give me half his income while his family went hungry. When I found out, we had quite a little talk, and at first he was offended. Finally, he saw that he was neglecting his own family, which is a tragic thing to do. It is amazing how people try to escape a responsibility in a pious way.

Ye hypocrites, well did Esaias prophesy of you saying,

This people draweth nigh unto me with their'mouth, and honoureth me with their lips; but their heart is far from me [Matt. 15:7–8].

The Lord called the scribes and Pharisees *hypocrites*. This is the most frightful word in Scripture. Nothing quite corresponds to it, but it did not have quite the meaning in that day that it does today. To us it is a scorching word, but in Jesus' day it simply meant to answer back and was used of an actor in a play. It means that an actor would receive a cue and then answer back. Jesus accused the scribes and Pharisees of playing at religion.

The religious leaders were eager to have people go through the ceremony of washing their hands, but they ignored the condition of the heart, which was the important thing to God. In a very pious way they were breaking the Mosaic Law.

My friend, we also are pretty good at rationalizing. Parents say to their children, "You wash your hands before you come to the table," but they pay no attention to what their children see on television, which is the thing that is damaging the heart. Oh, of course, children should wash their hands, but what is on the inside is far more important.

Now our Lord will enlarge upon that statement—

And he called the multitude, and said unto them, Hear, and understand:

Not that which goeth into the mouth defileth a man; but that which cometh out of the mouth, this defileth a man [Matt. 15:10–11].

The great principle that Jesus was teaching is that moral defilement is spiritual, not physical.

Then came his disciples, and said unto him, Knowest thou that the Pharisees were offended, after they heard this saying? [Matt. 15:12].

The disciples are amazed that the Lord would offend the Pharisees. Up to this point there has been conflict between the religious leaders and Jesus, but this is the breaking point. The Lord continues to instruct His disciples.

But he answered and said, Every plant, which My heavenly Father hath not planted, shall be rooted up [Matt. 15:13].

The word *plant* here means "system". It is not too broad to interpret Jesus as saying, "Every religious system which My heavenly Father hath not planted shall be rooted up."

Let them alone: they be blind leaders of the blind. And if the blind lead the blind, both shall fall into the ditch [Matt. 15:14].

This to me is a humorous statement, and it is certainly biting sarcasm. The Pharisees were the blind leaders.

Then answered Peter and said unto him, Declare unto us this parable [Matt. 15:15].

The Lord has been speaking in parables to His disciples, but they had not gotten His point yet.

And Jesus said, Are ye also yet without understanding?

Do not ye yet understand, that whatsoever entereth in at the mouth goeth into the belly, and is cast out into the draught?

> **But those things which proceed out of the mouth come forth from the heart; and they defile the man [Matt. 15:16-18].**

This is a great principle. A person is not defiled by what goes into his mouth but by what comes out of his mouth. As someone has well said, what is in the well of the heart will come up in the bucket of the mouth sooner or later. Listen to Him—

> **For out of the heart proceed evil thoughts, murders, adulteries, fornications, thefts, false witness, blasphemies:**
>
> **These are the things which defile a man: but to eat with unwashen hands defileth not a man [Matt. 15:19-20].**

We are certainly seeing this working out in our contemporary culture. We are in the period of the "new morality" and have reached the day that Isaiah talked about when he said that they would ". . . call evil good, and good evil . . ." (Isa. 5:20). Those of us who believe the Bible are considered squares and entirely wrong. What do we have in this day of freedom, now that the lid has been taken off and man expresses what is in his heart? Do we have a new *morality*? No, we have the same old things—evil thoughts, murder, adultery, fornication, false witness, blasphemy, and thefts. We have really opened a Pandora's box, and we are in trouble.

Man has to be *controlled*. He is the most vicious animal on earth. We put other animals in cages, but man must be free to do his thing, and our Lord has told us what mankind will do, and He says that these things *defile*. All about us today is an emphasis on sex—in our schools, even in our churches, on television, on radio; it stares at you from billboards, from the covers of magazines, from newspaper headlines. My friend, these things *defile*. Don't tell me that you are immune to it; no one is immune to this type of thing. Our children and young people are being *defiled*—all in the lofty-sounding terminology of freedom of speech! The things that are in the heart are now coming out. Our Lord has made a tremendous statement here.

JESUS HEALS THE SYROPHOENICIAN WOMAN'S DAUGHTER

Then Jesus went thence, and departed into the coasts of Tyre and Sidon [Matt. 15:21].

Now our Lord leaves the land of Israel for the first time during His public ministry. This is interesting because He came to Israel as her King. When He sent His disciples out, He instructed them to go into the cities of Israel but not beyond her boundaries. Then the Lord was rejected by Israel, and there arose conflict. The breaking point between Jesus and the religious rulers came only a few verses ago. What happens? Jesus Himself steps over the boundaries of Israel and lays down another great principle. He will now receive the Gentiles. His invitation is, "Come unto me, all ye that labour and are heavy laden, and I will give you rest [lit., "rest you"]" (Matt. 11:28).

And, behold, a woman of Canaan came out of the same coasts, and cried unto him, saying, Have mercy on me, O Lord, thou son of David; my daughter is grievously vexed with a devil.

But he answered her not a word. And his disciples came and besought him, saying, Send her away; for she crieth after us [Matt. 15:22–23].

The Syrophoenician woman was a mixture of several races and a true Gentile (see Mark 7:26 for her nationality). She had no claim on Jesus as the Son of David, and when she addressed Him as such, He answered her not a word.

The disciples said, "Send her away, for she crieth after us." She was causing a disturbance and probably a little embarrassment.

But he answered and said, I am not sent but unto the lost sheep of the house of Israel [Matt. 15:24].

This seems to be a harsh statement, but it was a statement of fact. Jesus was offering Himself first as the fulfillment of all the prophecies concerning the coming of the King in David's line. He was forcing this gentile woman to recognize that fact.

Jesus came as King of the Jews. You mark that down—it was the primary issue that had to be settled. He died with this superscription written over Him on the Cross: THIS IS JESUS THE KING OF THE JEWS.

Now listen to this gentile woman—

> **Then came she and worshipped him, saying, Lord, help me [Matt. 15:25].**

When she addressed Him as the Son of David, He said, "I am not sent but unto the lost sheep of the house of Israel." She as a Gentile had no claim upon Him as the Son of David. However, now she comes and worships Him, calling Him "Lord", and asks for help. Now she will get help, as we shall see.

> **But he answered and said, It is not meet to take the children's bread, and to cast it to dogs [Matt. 15:26].**

That is a very strong statement! Such a rebuff would have driven many of us away. We would have turned on our heels and said, "You can't talk to us like that!"

> **And she said, Truth, Lord: yet the dogs eat of the crumbs which fall from their masters' table [Matt. 15:27].**

You remember that our Lord told of a poor man who ate of the crumbs that fell from a rich man's table and the dogs came and licked his sores. The Israelites used the word *dog* in reference to the Gentiles. This woman was willing to bear that reproach because she believed in the Lord Jesus.

Then Jesus answered and said unto her, O woman, great
is thy faith: be it unto thee even as thou wilt. And her
daughter was made whole from that very hour [Matt.
15:28].

Our Lord really marveled at the faith of this gentile woman. He had
said, "Come unto me, all ye that labor and are heavy laden—I'll help
you; I'll lift your burden," and that is what He did even for a Canaan-
ite. Her answer had revealed a great faith, and to that our Lord re-
sponded.

JESUS CONTINUES TO HEAL

And Jesus departed from thence, and came nigh unto
the sea of Galilee; and went up into a mountain, and sat
down there.

And great multitudes came unto him, having with them
those that were lame, blind, dumb, maimed, and many
others, and cast them down at Jesus' feet; and he healed
them [Matt. 15:29–30].

Again I call your attention to the multitudes of folk whom Jesus
healed. There were not just a few isolated cases that could not be sub-
stantiated, but there were so many that nobody denied He performed
miracles of healing.

Insomuch that the multitude wondered, when they saw
the dumb to speak, the maimed to be whole, the lame to
walk, and the blind to see: and they glorified the God of
Israel [Matt. 15:31].

JESUS FEEDS THE FOUR THOUSAND

This miracle seems to be almost a duplication of the feeding of the
five thousand.

> Then Jesus called his disciples unto him, and said, I
> have compassion on the multitude, because they con-
> tinue with me now three days, and have nothing to eat:
> and I will not send them away fasting, lest they faint in
> the way [Matt. 15:32].

Note again His compassion for people.

> And his disciples say unto him, Whence should we have
> so much bread in the wilderness, as to fill so great a
> multitude? [Matt. 15:33].

Let's not miss the message that is here. Frankly, it seems like just a
rerun of the feeding of the five thousand. It appears to be a repetition,
and we wonder why Matthew included it since it doesn't seem to add
any further advancement of the messianic claims of the Lord Jesus.
However, we are in the section in which the emphasis is no longer
upon Jesus pressing His messianic claim but the emphasis is on the
rejection of His claim. And this miracle shows how slow the disciples
were to learn. They had already witnessed the feeding of the five thousand, and I think it took place only a few days before this; yet here
they raise the same old objections of unbelief. Again His disciples
say to Him, "Whence should we have so much bread in the wilderness, as to fill so great a multitude?"

> And Jesus saith unto them, How many loaves have ye?
> And they said, Seven, and a few little fishes.
>
> And he commanded the multitude to sit down on the
> ground.
>
> And he took the seven loaves and the fishes, and gave
> thanks, and brake them, and gave to his disciples, and
> the disciples to the multitude [Matt. 15:34–36].

Again He fed the multitudes. This is a revelation that the disciples had
not really learned the lesson. Their reluctance to believe actually con-

stitutes a form of rejection. My friend, unbelief is sin. In Romans 14:23 it says that ". . . whatsoever is not of faith is sin." In Hebrews 12:1 we are admonished to ". . . lay aside every weight, and the sin which doth so easily beset us. . . ." What is that weight? I think it is unbelief. Unbelief is sin. I am willing to make this confession: I wish that I believed Him more. He is worthy to be believed; I ought to believe Him fully, but the problem is with me. And I suspect that the problem is with you, also.

The Lord Jesus fed the multitude—

> **And they did all eat, and were filled: and they took up of the broken meat that was left seven baskets full.**
>
> **And they that did eat were four thousand men, beside women and children [Matt. 15:37–38].**

Notice that it was four thousand men plus women and children. In other words, families were there. Again, if we put one woman and one child with each man, the total fed would be twelve thousand.

> **And he sent away the multitude, and took ship, and came into the coasts of Magdala [Matt. 15:39].**

This was part of the Lord's Galilean ministry. Magdala is on the Sea of Galilee and today lies in ruins.

This chapter reveals that our Lord's disciples are not keeping up. They are slow to believe and slow to understand. This is actually hindering the Lord Jesus. It seems at this point that, since He has reached the breaking point with the religious rulers, He is having a real problem with His disciples. He appears to be just marking time until they catch up.

Frankly, He is very patient with you and me, also. Many of us need to catch up; we are far behind in our belief and understanding. Oh, that we might believe Him!

CHAPTER 16

THEME: Jesus continues the conflict with the Pharisees and Sadducees; Jesus calls for a confession from His disciples, and Peter speaks for the group; Jesus confronts them for the first time with the church, His death and resurrection

THE PHARISEES AND SADDUCEES ASK FOR A SIGN

For the second time the Pharisees and Sadducees ask for a sign from heaven, and again they are referred to Jonah.

The Pharisees also with the Sadducees came, and tempting desired him that he would shew them a sign from heaven.

He answered and said unto them, When it is evening, ye say, It will be fair weather: for the sky is red.

And in the morning, It will be foul weather to-day: for the sky is red and lowering. O ye hypocrites, ye can discern the face of the sky; but can ye not discern the signs of the times? [Matt. 16:1–3].

In Matthew 12:38 the scribes and Pharisees asked for a sign. At that time the Lord gave them the sign of Jonah. He is going to do that again, but first He calls their attention to the fact that, although they are very good at predicting the weather, they don't seem to be able to recognize the signs of the times.

Actually, the religious rulers are trying to trap the Lord Jesus, and He is going to warn His own men to beware of them. Notice that this is the second time He calls them "O ye hypocrites."

A wicked and adulterous generation seeketh after a sign; and there shall no sign be given unto it, but the

sign of the prophet Jonas. And he left them, and departed [Matt. 16:4].

Our Lord had provided them with many signs, but they would not accept them. For the second time He predicts the sign of Jonah ("Jonas" is the Greek form of the Hebrew name *Jonah*). Back in chapter 12 verse 40 He had said, "For as Jonas was three days and three nights in the whale's belly; so shall the Son of man be three days and three nights in the heart of the earth." These Pharisees and Sadducees were not about to accept that as a sign.

In this chapter we will see three viewpoints concerning Jesus. The Pharisees and Sadducees consider Him an imposter and do not believe that He is the Messiah. The multitude thinks He is John the Baptist, Elijah, Jeremiah, or another of the prophets. In this, they were complimentary, although they missed the mark completely. His disciples present the third viewpoint. They believe that Jesus is the Messiah (Christ), the Son of the living God.

The Pharisees and Sadducees were asking for a sign. Jesus said that no sign would be given them but the sign of the prophet Jonah. "And he left them and departed." There is a note of finality in His action as He turns and walks away from them. Then He warns His disciples of the leaven of these religious rulers.

JESUS WARNS HIS DISCIPLES

And when his disciples were come to the other side, they had forgotten to take bread.

Then Jesus said unto them, Take heed and beware of the leaven of the Pharisees and of the Sadducees.

And they reasoned among themselves, saying, It is because we have taken no bread [Matt. 16:5–7].

In Matthew 13 we learned that leaven is *always* a principle of evil and never a principle of good. The Lord says to beware of the leaven. If you are cautioned to beware of something, it will not be welcome or good.

The disciples missed the understanding of the leaven at first, thinking it was bread.

> **Which when Jesus perceived, he said unto them, O ye of little faith, why reason ye among yourselves, because ye have brought no bread?**
>
> **Do ye not yet understand, neither remember the five loaves of the five thousand, and how many baskets ye took up?**
>
> **Neither the seven loaves of the four thousand, and how many baskets ye took up?**
>
> **How is it that ye do not understand that I spake it not to you concerning bread, that ye should beware of the leaven of the Pharisees and of the Sadducees?**
>
> **Then understood they how that he bade them not beware of the leaven of bread, but of the doctrine of the Pharisees and of the Sadducees [Matt. 16:8–12].**

If it were a matter of material bread, the disciples should have remembered the two miracles of His—providing food for the five thousand and the four thousand—but it was not a matter of material bread. Leaven, according to our Lord's interpretation, is false *doctrine*. It is that which is evil. When people speak about the "leaven of the gospel," they are using a contradiction of terms. Leaven is never a picture of the gospel. Leaven always is symbolic of evil. If you accept the Lord Jesus Christ as an authority, this ought to clarify once and for all what leaven represents.

JESUS CALLS FOR A CONFESSION OF HIMSELF

All the way through the Gospel of Matthew we need to keep our thinking caps on because this Gospel is the key to the rest of the Scriptures. We need to make sharp distinctions and note carefully what happens.

When Jesus came into the coasts of Caesarea Philippi,
he asked his disciples, saying, Whom do men say that I
the Son of man am? [Matt. 16:13].

If you look on a map, you will find three Caesareas. Caesarea Philippi
is located to the north of the Sea of Galilee. The Lord Jesus is in the
north, and He is in a position from which He is going to turn and
begin a movement directly toward Jerusalem and the Cross. Before He
begins that journey, there are two things that must be clear in the
minds of His disciples: (1) who He is, and (2) what He is going to do.
My friend, these are the two things that all of us have to be clear on in
order to be Christians. We have to know who He is, and we have to
know what He did. We need to know these things in order that we
might exercise faith and be saved.

Note our Lord's first question: "Whom do men say that I the Son of
man am?" This is a question which He is still asking, and it is a question that is still being answered in our day. He still is the most contro-
versial Person who has ever lived on the topside of this earth. Now we
will hear the viewpoint of the multitudes, the crowds that followed
Him. I believe that if you or I asked this question on a street corner of
our own towns, we would probably get similar answers because folk
are still confused about Him.

And they said, Some say that thou art John the Baptist:
some, Elias; and others, Jeremias, or one of the prophets
[Matt. 16:14].

"Some say that thou art John the Baptist." John the Baptist was a great
man, and the people recognized him as such. In our day there are
many folk who say that Jesus was a great teacher.

Some said regarding Jesus that He was "Elias". (The name *Elias*
was the Greek form of "Elijah".) Elijah was certainly a great person,
and there are those in our day who say that Jesus was a great person.

"And others, Jeremias." (Again, the Greek form is used.) Jeremiah
was the weeping prophet, and the people saw our Lord weep. The
crowds gave Him the credit for being a great prophet.

"Or one of the prophets." I suppose there was a variety of viewpoints as to which prophet Jesus was.

These, then, were the viewpoints of the average persons of that day.

A young preacher friend of mine, an extrovert, heard me speak of this; so he went out on the street corners and asked the question concerning Jesus Christ of folk who passed by. He got all sorts of viewpoints. Some said that He was the greatest teacher this world has ever seen. One person said that He was a founder of religion. Another felt that He was a good man. Another put Him in a class with other men who were famous in history—just "one of the prophets," you see.

Now the Lord Jesus turns to His apostles and asks them—

He saith unto them, But whom say ye that I am?

And Simon Peter answered and said, Thou art the Christ, the Son of the living God [Matt. 16:15–16].

The time has come for the disciples to make a decision and render a confession. Simon Peter was evidently the spokesman for the group. He said, "Thou art the Christ," which meant the Messiah, the Anointed One, the One who was predicted in the Old Testament, and the Lord Jesus was the fulfillment. Also—"the Son of the living God." Up to this point, that was the best confession and the highest tribute that could be made to Him. This is who Jesus is!

And Jesus answered and said unto him, Blessed art thou, Simon Bar-jona: for flesh and blood hath not revealed it unto thee, but my Father which is in heaven [Matt. 16:17].

Only the Holy Spirit can make Christ known to any person. No man today can call Jesus "Lord" but by the Holy Spirit. Only the Spirit of God can take the things of Christ and reveal them to us. Jesus said, "Flesh and blood hath not revealed it unto thee"; that is, "You didn't learn it by being with Me." I hear folk say, "Well, if I could have been with Jesus for three years [the apostles had been with Him about two and one half years now], then I would really know who He is." Would you? My friend, you can know Him just as well today because the Spirit of God has to make Him real to you.

And I say also unto thee, That thou art Peter, and upon this rock I will build my church; and the gates of hell shall not prevail against it [Matt. 16:18].

Let us look at this verse carefully. On what rock did Jesus build His church? There are those who say that it was built on Simon Peter. Well, obviously it was not, because there is a play upon words here. In the original Greek it is, "Thou art *Petros* [a little piece of rock], and upon this *petra* [bedrock] I will build my church." There are others who hold that Christ is building His church upon the confession that Simon Peter made. I don't agree with that at all.

Who is the Rock? The Rock is Christ. The church is built upon Christ. We have Simon Peter's own explanation of this. In 1 Peter 2:4, referring to Christ, he writes, "To whom coming, as unto a living stone, disallowed indeed of men, but chosen of God, and precious." And he remembers Isaiah 28:16, ". . . Behold, I lay in Sion a chief corner stone, elect, precious: and he that believeth on him shall not be confounded" (1 Pet. 2:6). The church is built upon Christ; He is the foundation. "For other foundation can no man lay than that is laid, which is Jesus Christ" (1 Cor. 3:11). Christ is the stone, and He says on this rock He *will build* His church. The church was still future when the Lord made this statement. And please don't tell me there was a church in the Old Testament because the church did not come into existence until after the death, resurrection, and ascension of Christ, and the sending of the Holy Spirit. There could not have been a church until all of these things had taken place. "I will build my church"— this was future.

The "gates of hell" refers to death. The word used for *hell* is the Greek word *hades*, the *sheol* of the Old Testament, which refers to the unseen world and means "death." The gates of *death* shall not prevail against Christ's church. One of these days the Lord Himself shall descend from heaven with a shout. That shout will be like the voice of an archangel and like a trumpet because the *dead* in Christ are to be raised. The gates of *death* shall not prevail against His church.

And I will give unto thee the keys of the kingdom of heaven: and whatsoever thou shalt bind on earth shall be bound in heaven: and whatsoever thou shalt loose on earth shall be loosed in heaven [Matt. 16:19].

What are the keys of the kingdom of heaven? Were they given only to Simon Peter? No, Jesus gives them to those who make the same confession made by Peter, those who know Christ as Savior. If you are a child of God, you have the keys as well as any person has the keys. The keys were the badge of authority of the office of the scribes who interpreted the Scriptures to the people (see Neh. 8:2–8). Every Christian today has the Scriptures and, therefore, the keys. If we withhold the Word, we "bind on earth"; if we give the Word, we "loose on earth." No man or individual church has the keys—to the exclusion of all other believers. We have a responsibility today to give out the gospel because it is the only thing that can save people. This is a tremendous revelation. Who is sufficient for these things? You and I have a responsibility that is awesome indeed!

Then charged he his disciples that they should tell no man that he was Jesus the Christ [Matt. 16:20].

The Lord made this request because the mere knowledge of who He is will not save you. To find salvation you must know who He is and what He did and accept Him by faith.

JESUS ANNOUNCES HIS DEATH AND RESURRECTION

For the first time the Lord Jesus announces to His disciples His death and resurrection. The time was approximately six months before He was actually crucified. Why did He wait so long to make such an important announcement? Obviously, His disciples were not prepared for it, even at this time, judging from their reaction. He repeated five times the fact that He was going to Jerusalem to die (Matt. 17:12; 17:22–23; 20:18–19; 20:28). In spite of this intensive instruction, the disciples failed to grasp the significance of it all until after His resurrection.

> **From that time forth began Jesus to shew unto his disciples, how that he must go unto Jerusalem, and suffer many things of the elders and chief priests and scribes, and be killed, and be raised again the third day [Matt. 16:21].**

This is what the Lord Jesus did for you and me. This is the gospel: that Christ died for our sins according to the Scriptures, was buried and raised again. You must know who He is. You must know what He did for you. If you know these two things, and by faith believe and receive them, you are saved. This had never been revealed before except to Nicodemus at the beginning of our Lord's ministry in John 3:1–16.

> **Then Peter took him, and began to rebuke him, saying, Be it far from thee, Lord: this shall not be unto thee [Matt. 16:22].**

In essence Peter said, "You are the Messiah; You are the Son of God. You must not, You *cannot* go to the cross!" The cross was not in the thinking of the apostles at all, as you can see.

> **But he turned, and said unto Peter, Get thee behind me, Satan: thou art an offence unto me: for thou savourest not the things that be of God, but those that be of men [Matt. 16:23].**

It is satanic for anyone to deny the facts of the gospel which are that Jesus died on the cross for our sins, was buried, and rose again from the dead. It is satanic when a man in the pulpit will deny these truths.

The substitutionary death of Christ is the only thing that can save us, my friend. Later on Peter wrote this: "Who his own self bare our sins in his own body on the tree, that we, being dead to sins, should live unto righteousness: by whose stripes ye were healed" (1 Pet. 2:24). My, what a transformation had taken place in the mind of Peter!

Our Lord said to Peter, "Get thee behind me, Satan." Imagine this: Here is Peter by whom the Spirit of God could say that Jesus was the Son of God, and yet he could in the next moment let Satan deceive him!

> **Then said Jesus unto his disciples, If any man will come after me, let him deny himself, and take up his cross, and follow me [Matt. 16:24].**

Many people interpret this verse, "Let him deny himself ice cream" or "Let him deny himself some luxury down here." What this verse says is "Let him deny *himself!*" You already know that the hardest person in the world to deny is yourself. To deny myself dessert is hard enough, but to deny *myself* is difficult indeed. To deny myself is to put self out of the picture and to put Christ in the place of self.

"And take up his cross, and follow me." We are not to take up Christ's Cross but our own cross. There is a cross for you and a cross for me—that is, if we are going to *follow* Him.

> **For whosoever will save his life shall lose it: and whosoever will lose his life for my sake shall find it.**
>
> **For what is a man profited, if he shall gain the whole world, and lose his own soul? or what shall a man give in exchange for his soul?**
>
> **For the Son of man shall come in the glory of his Father with his angels; and then he shall reward every man according to his works [Matt. 16:25–27].**

The person who will not assume the risks involved in becoming a disciple of the Lord Jesus Christ will, in the long run, lose his life eternally. The opposite is also true. At Christ's second coming all accounts will be settled and everyone will receive his proper rewards.

Verily I say unto you, There be some standing here, which shall not taste of death, till they see the Son of man coming in his kingdom [Matt. 16:28].

This verse belongs with chapter 17 because the account of the transfiguration of Jesus explains what He meant when He made this statement.

CHAPTER 17

THEME: The Transfiguration; the demon-possessed boy and the faithless disciples; Jesus pays taxes by performing a miracle

THE TRANSFIGURATION

As we noted at the conclusion of chapter 16, the final verse belongs to this chapter because it explains what our Lord meant when He made this statement:

> **Verily I say unto you, There be some standing here, which shall not taste of death, till they see the Son of man coming in his kingdom [Matt. 16:28].**

This was fulfilled for the apostles in the transfiguration of Jesus. The Transfiguration is that picture of the Son of man coming in His Kingdom. Someone may say, "Can you be sure that the Lord Jesus had reference to His coming Transfiguration?" Well, Simon Peter was one of the apostles who was present at the Transfiguration, and in his second epistle he wrote of that experience: "For we have not followed cunningly devised fables, when we made known unto you the power and coming of our Lord Jesus Christ, but were eyewitnesses of his majesty. For he received from God the Father honour and glory, when there came such a voice to him from the excellent glory, This is my beloved Son, in whom I am well pleased. And this voice which came from heaven we heard, when we were with him in the holy mount" (2 Pet. 1:16–18). How was Jesus' statement fulfilled for the apostles in that day? When the Lord Jesus Christ was glorified on the Mount of Transfiguration with three of His disciples present, this statement was fulfilled. The Transfiguration was a miniature picture of the Kingdom, and Simon Peter confirmed this for us.

The other Gospels give the account of the Transfiguration, with the exception of the Gospel of John. This leads me to say something that may startle you. The Transfiguration does not prove, nor set forth, the deity of Christ. It sets forth the *humanity* of Christ. The Gospel of John emphasizes the deity of Christ and therefore omits the account of the Transfiguration, although the other three Gospels record it.

The transfiguration of the Lord Jesus Christ is, in my judgment, not only the proof of His humanity but the *hope* of humanity. The Man whom you see glorified there, transfigured, is the kind of person that you, my friend, will be someday if you are a child of God. "Beloved, now are we the sons of God, and it doth not yet appear what we shall be: but we know that, when he shall appear, we shall be like him; for we shall see him as he is" (1 John 3:2). The glorious prospect of being like Christ is before every man.

The Lord Jesus Christ was glorified before His death and resurrection, and this is the picture which is given to us here. You will find that the Gospel of Luke presents details which neither Matthew nor Mark include, because Dr. Luke is the one who sets forth the perfect humanity of Jesus.

And after six days Jesus taketh Peter, James, and John his brother, and bringeth them up into an high mountain apart,

And was transfigured before them: and his face did shine as the sun, and his raiment was white as the light [Matt. 17:1–2].

"His face did shine as the sun." The light shone from within Him rather than upon Him from the outside like a spotlight. At this point let me make the suggestion that perhaps it was this sort of thing that clothed Adam and Eve in the Garden of Eden before their fall. After they sinned, they discovered that they were naked. The implication is that they were not naked before, which leads me to believe that they were clothed with this type of light. And it was the *humanity* of Jesus that was transfigured. The Transfiguration sets forth His perfect humanity.

The word *transfigured* is a very interesting word. It is the word *metamorphosis*, which means "a change of form or structure." The little woolly caterpillar will someday become a beautiful butterfly by the process of metamorphosis. This body that I have today, filled with infirmity and cancer, will someday be transfigured, and even those who are alive at the coming of Christ will be changed, transfigured. This is the hope of humanity.

And, behold, there appeared unto them Moses and Elias talking with him [Matt. 17:3].

Moses was the representative of the Law, and Elijah was the representative of the prophets. Moses had died, and Elijah had departed from this world in a chariot of fire. Luke tells us they were discussing Jesus' decease in Jerusalem—"And, behold, there talked with him two men, which were Moses and Elias: Who appeared in glory, and spake of his decease which he should accomplish at Jerusalem" (Luke 9:30–31). The Law and the prophets bore testimony to the death of the Lord Jesus Christ.

Then answered Peter, and said unto Jesus, Lord, it is good for us to be here: if thou wilt, let us make here three tabernacles; one for thee, and one for Moses, and one for Elias [Matt. 17:4].

Simon Peter could never resist an opportunity to make a speech. Every occasion was an auspicious one for him. He generally got to his feet to say something, and usually it was to say the wrong thing—that is, until the Day of Pentecost. But here it is the wrong thing; he should have kept quiet. God Himself rebukes him, as we shall see, because he was attempting to place Moses and Elijah on the same plane with the Lord Jesus. Luke offers the explanation for this indiscretion of Peter's by stating, " . . . not knowing what he said" (Luke 9:33). And there are a lot of folk who talk without knowing what they are saying! Peter was rebuked. He should have kept still.

> **While he yet spake, behold, a bright cloud overshadowed them: and behold a voice out of the cloud, which said, This is my beloved Son, in whom I am well pleased; hear ye him [Matt. 17:5].**

This is God the Father's testimony to Jesus, the Son. Jesus is the final authority in matters of revelation. What Moses, Elijah and the prophets had to say was wonderful. The writer to the Hebrews says: "God, who at sundry times and in divers manners spake in time past unto the fathers by the prophets, Hath in these last days spoken unto us by his Son . . ." (Heb. 1:1–2). The Son is the One who came to earth as the final revelation of God to man.

Now notice this great statement by the Father—"This is my beloved Son, in whom I am well pleased; hear ye him." Have you ever heard a voice out of heaven commending you and saying that God was well pleased with you? Well, He has never said that to me either. In fact, He has never said it to anyone but this One. The Lord Jesus is the only One who ever has been well pleasing to God. And you and I well never get into God's presence until we are in Christ by faith. When we receive Christ as our Savior, then we are placed in the body of believers. Christ is the only One in whom God has been pleased, and we are accepted in the Beloved.

> **And when the disciples heard it, they fell on their face, and were sore afraid.**
>
> **And Jesus came and touched them, and said, Arise, and be not afraid.**
>
> **And when they had lifted up their eyes, they saw no man, save Jesus only [Matt. 17:6–8].**

Do you want a good motto for your life? I suggest these two words: *Jesus only.* He is the One who is the authority. I hope you will mark those two words, *Jesus only,* in your Bible. They provide a good motto for all of us.

And as they came down from the mountain, Jesus charged them, saying, Tell the vision to no man, until the Son of man be risen again from the dead [Matt. 17:9].

Why wait until the Resurrection to tell it, and why should it be told at that time? Because it is part of the gospel story. It tells who Jesus is. He is the perfect Lamb of God. He has been tested for three years, and at this time He is on the way to the Cross to die for the sins of the world. You see, God required a lamb without blemish, and the Lord Jesus Christ is the only One who could die a substitutionary death for mankind, because He was sinless. In His perfect humanity He was transfigured. He is the *hope* of mankind.

The hope of mankind is not in science or education. Both of them are letting us down today. They have created Frankenstein monsters, and we don't know what to do with them. For example, they have invented a little gasoline buggy in Detroit, Michigan, that is giving us a lot of trouble by polluting the air and clogging all the highways. Science cannot solve the problem. Believe me, friend, the hope of the world just happens to be in a person by the name of Jesus Christ. Be sure you know Him; He is your only hope.

And his disciples asked him, saying, Why then say the scribes that Elias must first come? [Matt. 17:10].

Now this is a remarkable statement—

And Jesus answered and said unto them, Elias truly shall first come, and restore all things [Matt. 17:11].

Jesus confirms what was said in the prophecy of Malachi.

But I say unto you, That Elias is come already, and they knew him not, but have done unto him whatsoever they listed. Likewise shall also the Son of man suffer of them [Matt. 17:12].

This raises a question in the minds of a great many folk regarding John the Baptist. Was he really Elijah? We have covered the same problem in Matthew 11. What our Lord is doing in this chapter is trying to forestall the argument that Jesus had to die on the cross because John the Baptist was not Elijah—and Elijah has to come before Christ returns to establish His Kingdom. Our Lord is saying that if they would receive Him as King, John would be Elijah. Don't ask me how that could be—I am only telling you what the Scriptures teach.

"Likewise shall also the Son of man suffer of them"—this is the second time the Lord Jesus mentions His approaching crucifixion.

> **Then the disciples understood that he spake unto them of John the Baptist [Matt. 17:13].**

THE DEMON-POSSESSED BOY

In this scene we have a Kingdom-of-Heaven situation, as it is in today's world. Where does the church fit into it? Go with me now to the foot of the mountain where the other disciples (who were not with the Lord on the Mount of Transfiguration) are really in trouble.

> **And when they were come to the multitude, there came to him a certain man, kneeling down to him, and saying,**
>
> **Lord, have mercy on my son: for he is lunatic, and sore vexed: for ofttimes he falleth into the fire, and oft into the water.**
>
> **And I brought him to thy disciples, and they could not cure him [Matt. 17:14–16].**

This was probably the worst case which had been brought to the attention of Jesus. It was also a sad situation because the disciples were impotent. This is a picture of the church today in a world that is demon-possessed and has gone crazy. Why is the church impotent in this crazy world? Because it doesn't have enough psychology or enough methods or enough money? It has all of those things, but they are not what the church really needs.

This man had to say to Jesus, "I brought him to Your disciples, but they could not heal him."

> **Then Jesus answered and said, O faithless and perverse generation, how long shall I be with you? how long shall I suffer you? bring him hither to me [Matt. 17:17].**

"O faithless and perverse generation" would be His word to the church in our day and probably individually to you and to me. "Bring him hither to me." Jesus is the Great Physician. Take your case to Him, my friend.

> **And Jesus rebuked the devil; and he departed out of him: and the child was cured from that very hour [Matt. 17:18].**

The Lord rebuked His disciples, and then He rebuked the demon. This is probably the worst case of demon possession our Lord dealt with.

> **Then came the disciples to Jesus apart, and said, Why could not we cast him out?**
>
> **And Jesus said unto them, Because of your unbelief: for verily I say unto you, If ye have faith as a grain of mustard seed, ye shall say unto this mountain, Remove hence to yonder place; and it shall remove; and nothing shall be impossible unto you [Matt. 17:19–20].**

"Nothing shall be impossible unto you"—that is, nothing that is according to the will of God for you. It was God's will that this boy be delivered from demon possession. Why couldn't the disciples deliver him? Because they didn't have the faith.

Howbeit this kind goeth not out but by prayer and fasting [Matt. 17:21].

This verse is not in the better manuscripts.

AGAIN JESUS ANNOUNCES HIS DEATH AND RESURRECTION

For the third time the Lord reminds His disciples that He would die and be raised again from the dead.

And while they abode in Galilee, Jesus said unto them, The Son of man shall be betrayed into the hands of men:

And they shall kill him, and the third day he shall be raised again. And they were exceeding sorry [Matt. 17:22–23].

This is the third time He speaks to His disciples of His death and resurrection. The first time He mentioned it was when they were in Caesarea Philippi. Now He is in Galilee, on His way to Jerusalem, and He mentions it again. All that the disciples can do is to feel sorry.

TAX MONEY FROM THE FISH'S MOUTH

And when they were come to Capernaum, they that received tribute money came to Peter, and said, Doth not your master pay tribute? [Matt. 17:24].

"Tribute" was the assessment collected annually for the support of the temple.

He saith, Yes. And when he was come into the house, Jesus prevented him, saying, What thinkest thou, Simon? of whom do the kings of the earth take custom or tribute? of their own children, or of strangers? [Matt. 17:25].

"Jesus prevented him" means that Jesus went before him.

> **Peter saith unto him, Of strangers. Jesus saith unto him,
> Then are the children free [Matt. 17:26].**

Jesus is tryng to show Peter that just as the royal family is exempt from tax, so He, as the Son of God, would not be obligated to pay for the support of God's house.

> **Notwithstanding, lest we should offend them, go thou to
> the sea, and cast an hook, and take up the fish that first
> cometh up; and when thou hast opened his mouth, thou
> shalt find a piece of money: that take, and give unto
> them for me and thee [Matt. 17:27].**

His method of getting the tax money was certainly novel, to say the least. Now our Lord demonstrates that He has recovered all that Adam lost. The creatures were obedient to Him. The fish as well as Peter followed His command. I believe that God had given to Adam the same dominion over all creation, but he lost it at the Fall. "And God said, Let us make man in our image, after our likeness: and let them have dominion over the fish of the sea, and over the fowl of the air, and over the cattle, and over all the earth, and over every creeping thing that creepeth upon the earth" (Gen. 1:26).

In the Transfiguration we see man restored to his original *purpose.* In the episode of the tribute money we see man restored to his original *performance.*

CHAPTER 18

THEME: *The little child, the lost sheep, conduct in the coming church, and the parable on forgiveness*

The next few chapters do not seem to further advance the movement in Matthew, but they do fill out many of the dark corners which have arisen because of the sudden digression in the Kingdom of Heaven due to the rejection of the King. Matthew 13 in the Mystery Parables Discourse has given us the overall outline of the Kingdom of Heaven in this age, but there are still questions to be answered. These chapters are helpful in answering many of them.

Now we find that the new birth is made essential in entering the kingdom.

A LITTLE CHILD BECOMES AN OBJECT LESSON

At the same time came the disciples unto Jesus, saying, Who is the greatest in the kingdom of heaven? [Matt. 18:1].

I wonder if you detect a note of fleshly ambition here. It may be that I just have a critical mind, but it seems to me that these men have been talking about this subject, and maybe two or three of them felt that they could reasonably be considered the greatest in the Kingdom of Heaven. So the Lord did a rather sensational thing.

And Jesus called a little child unto him, and set him in the midst of them [Matt. 18:2].

What does this tell us? It tells us that the little child came to the Lord without hesitation. In Mark 10:14 the Lord said, ". . . Suffer the little children to come unto me, and forbid them not. . . ." The problem was not in getting the little children to come to Him but in stopping the adults from hindering the little ones in coming to the Lord. This is a lovely picture we have here. Our Lord takes this little child and puts him in the midst of them.

And said, Verily I say unto you, Except ye be converted, and become as little children, ye shall not enter into the kingdom of heaven [Matt. 18:3].

This is a verse that has certainly been abused and misunderstood, but remember, the Lord Jesus is talking about *conversion* not *reversion*. Some people think this verse means that you must revert back to your childhood in some unusual fashion or that you are to become juvenile in your actions in order to enter the Kingdom of Heaven. The Lord is not talking about going back to a former childhood, but rather of going on to a new life. Here our Lord gives logic to the thinking of the disciples as He diverts their attention from the matter of holding an exalted place in the Kingdom to that of primary importance; namely, of first being able to secure entrance into that Kingdom. This is as radical as John 3:3, "Jesus answered and said unto him, Verily, verily, I say unto thee, Except a man be born again, he cannot see the kingdom of God." The important thing emphasized in this verse is the new birth. You must become a little child in the sense that you must be born again. When you are born again, you start out spiritually as a child.

Unfortunately, there are many folk who do not recognize their spiritual immaturity. When I was pastoring a large city church, you would be surprised at the number of requests that came to me from so-called new converts who wanted to come and give their testimonies. I feel that it was basically the same thing as the disciples' argument as to who would be the greatest in the Kingdom of Heaven. Our Lord says that if you have been converted, think of your spiritual age. You are to become a little child. Should a little child get up and blabber out a testimony immediately? Should a little child be an officer in the church? In listing qualifications for the office of bishop in the church, Paul rules out the novice: "Not a novice, lest being lifted up with pride he fall into the condemnation of the devil" (1 Tim. 3:6). I think that our Lord is saying something like that here.

> **Whosoever therefore shall humble himself as this little child, the same is greatest in the kingdom of heaven [Matt. 18:4].**

When you go back and emphasize the *entrance* into the Kingdom, the new birth, then you find that the one who humbles himself as a little child is the one who is greatest in the Kingdom.

> **And whoso shall receive one such little child in my name receiveth me.**
>
> **But whoso shall offend one of these little ones which believe in me, it were better for him that a millstone were hanged about his neck, and that he were drowned in the depth of the sea [Matt. 18:5–6].**

The word *offend* means "to cause to stumble"; that is, to lead into sin. Jesus warns against it in strong language! It seems to me that what He is doing in this section is making the evangelism of children a divine imperative. He gives top priority to winning the children to Christ. I commend anyone who is working with children today. There is nothing as important as that.

The story is told of Dwight L. Moody concerning his coming home one night after a meeting. His family asked him how many converts he had that night, and he said, "Two and a half." His family said, "Oh, you had two adults and one child who accepted the Lord as Savior." Moody replied, "No, no, two children and one adult accepted the Lord." He continued, "The adult was an old man and he had only half a life to give. He was just half of a convert." The little children are important.

A pastor of a Scottish church turned in his resignation years ago, and as he did so, the elders asked him why. "Well," he replied, "for this past year I've had but one convert, wee Bobby Moffat." Bobby Moffat was the man who opened up Africa to missionary work. It was the biggest year that preacher ever had! In these verses the Lord is putting a great emphasis upon children.

> Woe unto the world because of offences! for it must
> needs be that offences come; but woe to that man by
> whom the offence cometh!
>
> Wherefore if thy hand or thy foot offend thee, cut them
> off, and cast them from thee: it is better for thee to enter
> into life halt or maimed, rather than having two hands
> or two feet to be cast into everlasting fire [Matt. 18:7–8].

I can't think of anything more harsh than this!

> And if thine eye offend thee, pluck it out, and cast it
> from thee: it is better for thee to enter into life with one
> eye, rather than having two eyes to be cast into hell fire.
>
> Take heed that ye despise not one of these little ones; for
> I say unto you, That in heaven their angels do always
> behold the face of my Father which is in heaven [Matt.
> 18:9–10].

Our Lord says that we are not to despise one of the little ones. When
one of them dies, his spirit goes immediately to be with God. All little
ones go to heaven, my friend. If you have lost a little one, knowing
this will be a great comfort to you. They go to heaven, not because
they are innocent or because they are yours, but they go to heaven
because Jesus *died* for them. That is what our Lord is talking about
here. "Don't offend them; don't despise them. Let them come to Me.
Even if they die, their spirits are going to be right there in the presence
of My Father." So many parents wonder about the eternal state of their
little ones.

King David knew about his. When his son by Bathsheba fell ill, he
was greatly exercised about the life of the child. We have the record of
this in 2 Samuel 12:15–23. He fasted and wept and lay all night upon
the earth. But when the child was dead, he arose, bathed, changed his
clothes, and went into the house of God and worshiped. His servants were baffled by his actions, and David's explanation was this
" . . . While the child was yet alive, I fasted and wept: for I said, Who

can tell whether GOD will be gracious to me, that the child may live? But now he is dead, wherefore should I fast? can I bring him back again? I shall go to him, but he shall not return to me." He had the confidence that one day he would be with him. This is a very precious truth. Many people have lost little ones, and I have lost a little one, also—my firstborn. She is buried here in Altadena in Southern California. Every now and then I go by there and put a few flowers on her grave. She's not there; she's with Him, but I go there because that is all I have left of her now. But someday, some golden tomorrow, I'm going to be there in heaven, and I am going to see my little one. She is saved. I have two children—one in heaven and one here on earth. I confess that I have worried more about the one here than the one in heaven. I know where my firstborn is, and someday I'll go to be with her.

The feeling of our Lord about children is very important to note, especially in our day when there are so many crimes committed against these little ones. Recently, I have been reading about a mother and a stepfather who left a precious little girl along the freeway. How shocking it was to read about this. They just wanted to get rid of her. Some folk believe there is no hell, but I want to say this: If there were no hell, there ought to be one for folk like that! And there is one. Our Lord uses the strongest language possible in warning us about offenses against children.

PARABLE OF THE LOST SHEEP

Now our Lord moves into the wonderful parable of the lost sheep.

For the Son of man is come to save that which was lost [Matt. 18:11].

This parable is different from the parable of the lost sheep in Luke 15. The key to this parable is the word save. In Luke 15 the emphasis is upon *finding* the lost, and in Matthew 18 it is upon *saving* the lost.

How think ye? if a man have an hundred sheep, and one of them be gone astray, doth he not leave the ninety and

> nine, and goeth into the mountains, and seeketh that
> which is gone astray?
>
> And if so be that he find it, verily I say unto you, he
> rejoiceth more of that sheep, than of the ninety and nine
> which went not astray [Matt. 18:12–13].

Notice how He closes this—He is still thinking in terms of the "little
ones."

> Even so it is not the will of your Father which is in
> heaven, that one of these little ones should perish [Matt.
> 18:14].

He will take care of them until they get to the age of accountability, but
you, parent, are responsible for leading them to Christ. I am afraid
that our school systems are using our children as guinea pigs for
humanistic philosophies. Young people are paying an awful price in
the contemporary schoolroom. My friend, we have a tremendous responsibility before God in this area.

PATTERN FOR CONDUCT IN THE CHURCH

> Moreover if thy brother shall trespass against thee, go
> and tell him his fault between thee and him alone: if he
> shall hear thee, thou hast gained thy brother [Matt.
> 18:15].

If he sins against you, you are to go to him. This verse is speaking of
sin committed by a believer. The obligation is upon the one who has
been injured to approach his brother who has offended him and not
vice versa.

> But if he will not hear thee, then take with thee one or
> two more, that in the mouth of two or three witnesses
> every word may be established.

> **And if he shall neglect to hear them, tell it unto the church: but if he neglect to hear the church, let him be unto thee as an heathen man and a publican [Matt. 18:16–17].**

There are some people who like to smother trouble and cover it up. This is not the way the Lord tells us to handle it. If there is a problem between two believers, it should be worked out in an amiable, peaceful, and quiet manner. If the individuals cannot work things out, take it to a group. If the group cannot work things out, the last resort is to take the problem to the church as the final authority. The Lord says in conclusion, concerning this subject:

> **Verily I say unto you, Whatsoever ye shall bind on earth shall be bound in heaven: and whatsoever ye shall loose on earth shall be loosed in heaven [Matt. 18:18].**

We have already studied the contents of this verse in Matthew 16:19, where we learned that if we withhold the Word, we "bind on earth"; if we give the Word of God to others, we "loose on earth."

> **Again I say unto you, That if two of you shall agree on earth as touching any thing that they shall ask, it shall be done for them of my Father which is in heaven.**

> **For where two or three are gathered together in my name, there am I in the midst of them [Matt. 18:19–20].**

"If two of you shall agree on earth as touching any thing." Does He mean that if we agree on *anything*, He will hear us? Yes, but notice the condition: "where two or three are gathered together in *my name*." He will hear any request which is given in Christ's name—that is, a request that Christ Himself would make. Or, we could say that asking in His *name* is asking in His *will*.

"Where two or three are gathered together in my name, there am I in the midst of them" is the simplest form of church government. As verse 19 is a new basis for prayer, verse 20 is the new basis for the visible church. The early church began there: "And they continued stedfastly in the apostles' doctrine and fellowship, and in breaking of bread, and in prayers" (Acts 2:42).

JESUS' NEW PROVISO FOR FORGIVENESS

Then came Peter to him, and said, Lord, how oft shall my brother sin against me, and I forgive him? till seven times? [Matt. 18:21].

Peter thought he was being magnanimous when he said this because two or three times was all you had to forgive according to the rabbis. Simon Peter was willing to forgive seven times. But Peter's generosity was parsimonious in comparison to the new estimation of Jesus—

Jesus saith unto him, I say not unto thee, Until seven times: but, Until seventy times seven [Matt. 18:22].

That is four hundred and ninety times! By that time, things might be pretty well worked out. If not, both of them would have reached old age to the extent that it wouldn't amount to much anyway! Four hundred and ninety times is going the limit—and that is the point our Lord is making.

Therefore is the kingdom of heaven likened unto a certain king, which would take account of his servants.

And when he had begun to reckon, one was brought unto him, which owed him ten thousand talents.

But forasmuch as he had not to pay, his lord commanded him to be sold, and his wife, and children, and all that he had, and payment to be made.

The servant therefore fell down, and worshipped him, saying, Lord, have patience with me, and I will pay thee all [Matt. 18:23–26].

I guess he was saying that he wanted to pay it back on the installment plan.

> **Then the lord of that servant was moved with compassion, and loosed him, and forgave him the debt [Matt. 18:27].**

I think our Lord is using an outlandish illustration here to prove His point. The amount of money that this servant owed his lord was about twelve million dollars. That is a lot of money to forgive anyone!

> **But the same servant went out, and found one of his fellow-servants, which owed him an hundred pence: and he laid hands on him, and took him by the throat, saying, Pay me that thou owest [Matt. 18:28].**

"An hundred pence" amounted to about seventeen dollars! Compare that to twelve million!

> **And his fellow-servant fell down at his feet, and besought him, saying, Have patience with me, and I will pay thee all.**
>
> **And he would not: but went and cast him into prison, till he should pay the debt.**
>
> **So when his fellow-servants saw what was done, they were very sorry, and came and told unto their lord all that was done.**
>
> **Then his lord, after that he had called him, said unto him, O thou wicked servant, I forgave thee all that debt, because thou desiredst me:**
>
> **Shouldest not thou also have had compassion on thy fellow-servant, even as I had pity on thee?**
>
> **And his lord was wroth, and delivered him to the tormentors, till he should pay all that was due unto him.**

So likewise shall my heavenly Father do also unto you, if ye from your hearts forgive not every one his brother their trespasses [Matt. 18:29–35].

This parable of the servant, who was forgiven but refused to forgive another, illustrates the *principle* of forgiveness. This is a new principle presented in this passage, but it is not quite the basis of forgiveness for believers which is set forth in Ephesians 4:32, "And be ye kind one to another, tenderhearted, forgiving one another, even as God for Christ's sake hath forgiven you." *Because* God has forgiven us, we are to forgive each other. If God forgave our sins in the same way we forgive others, none of us would be forgiven. But after we have become children of God, because we have been forgiven, we are to forgive. This is the principle of Christian conduct, of course.

CHAPTER 19

THEME: Jesus enters Judea; proclaims God's standard for marriage and only grounds for divorce given; blesses little children; meets a rich young ruler; appoints the apostles to their position in the coming Kingdom

In the movement in Matthew, our attention is now directed to the geography of the gospel. Jesus again enters Judea as He moves to Jerusalem for the last time before His crucifixion. There is definite intention in all that He does and says.

JESUS RE-ENTERS JUDEA

And it came to pass, that when Jesus had finished these sayings, he departed from Galilee, and came into the coasts of Judaea beyond Jordan [Matt. 19:1].

"When Jesus had finished these sayings"—what sayings? The ones we have been considering in chapters 16—18. Having finished what He wanted to say in Galilee, He moved south and came into the borders of Judea, beyond Jordan, meaning the east bank of the Jordan River. The movement is in a physical and geographical sense now. Up yonder in Caesarea Philippi He announced that He was going to Jerusalem to die. He moved down into Galilee, and He spent time in that area around the Sea of Galilee. Capernaum was His headquarters, and He even crossed over into Gadara. Now He is on the border of Judea.

And great multitudes followed him; and he healed them there [Matt. 19:2].

I want to put two words together and emphasize what has been emphasized before several times. One word is *multitudes* and the other word is *healed*. It was not just a few people that were healed; multitudes were healed. I am more and more impressed by this as time goes on. If you are going to be a faith healer, brother, you ought to go to the hospitals and empty them. That is what our Lord did when He passed by; if anyone wanted to be healed, they could be healed. Multitudes were healed!

MARRIAGE AND DIVORCE

Now the religious rulers come to Him with a question regarding divorce. Our Lord restates God's ideal for marriage and the grounds for divorce.

The Pharisees also came unto him, tempting him, and saying unto him, Is it lawful for a man to put away his wife for every cause? [Matt. 19:3].

The Pharisees came to tempt or to *test* Him. They were after Him, trying to put Him in opposition to the Mosaic system. They brought a problem which is just as difficult today as it was then. "Is it lawful for a man to put away [divorce] his wife for every cause?" That is an equally live issue among Christians in our day.

Let me preface this a little by saying that God has given to all of mankind certain things for the welfare of the human family. For instance, He has given marriage for the protection of the home. Marriage is something which God has given to be a blessing to mankind whether saved or unsaved. Another example is that of capital punishment which God gave for the protection of a nation, to protect the lives of its citizens. Also God gave the sabbath law for the protection of the individual, that he might have one day of rest. God gave these laws to protect the individual, the family, and the nation. These were general laws which He gave to all mankind. Later on, He made them specific for His chosen people.

Now let's look at this question concerning marriage. Here it is in the smaller context of the nation Israel, of course. And we look at it today in the light of the contemporary Christian. "Is it lawful for a man to put away his wife for every cause?"

> **And he answered and said unto them, Have ye not read, that he which made them at the beginning made them male and female [Matt. 19:4].**

The Lord Jesus took them back to the very beginning, back to God's ideal of marriage.

The Mosaic Law had permitted divorce on a broad basis: "When a man hath taken a wife, and married her, and it come to pass that she find no favour in his eyes, because he hath found some uncleanness in her: then let him write her a bill of divorcement, and give it in her hand, and send her out of his house" (Deut. 24:1).

As far as the Mosaic Law was concerned, a divorce was not as bad as was marriage to a stranger. For instance, if the priest's daughter married a stranger, she was shut out from the nation Israel. However, as time went on, the Mosaic Law was made meaningless, and the granting of divorce was done on the flimsiest pretexts, such as burning the bread. As a result, there was a great deal of discussion relative to divorce in our Lord's day.

> **And said, For this cause shall a man leave father and mother, and shall cleave to his wife: and they twain shall be one flesh?**
>
> **Wherefore they are no more twain, but one flesh. What therefore God hath joined together, let not man put asunder [Matt. 19:5–6].**

This was God's original plan for man and woman before sin entered the human family. Divorce was not in God's original plan. Why? Because sin was not in God's original plan, and divorce is always a result of sin. Regardless of what you may say, there is sin in the relationship somewhere which causes divorce. So our Lord took them back to the original plan of God.

> **They say unto him, Why did Moses then command to give a writing of divorcement, and to put her away? [Matt. 19:7].**

You ought to read Deuteronomy 24:1–4 to get the background for their question. Why did Moses permit divorce?

> **He saith unto them, Moses because of the hardness of your hearts suffered you to put away your wives: but from the beginning it was not so [Matt. 19:8].**

Why did Moses permit it? Because of the hardness of their hearts. You see, marriage was given to mankind, and it is the tenderest and the sweetest of human relationships. There is nothing like it. And, actually, marriage was to represent the relationship between Christ and the church. Therefore, only believers can set forth this high and holy relationship. However, when they fail, and bitterness and hardness of heart enter in, then that marriage becomes a hollow sham, and it is just a mockery of marriage. My friend, marriage is made either in heaven or in hell—there is no third place to make it. When marriage is made in the wrong place, it is in trouble to begin with. Even Christians find that marriage becomes a very shaky proposition.

Because of the hardness of the human heart, God permitted divorce. God is merciful to us—oh, how merciful! But His ideal is never divorce. I recognize that we are living in a culture which is very lax in this area. There are multitudes of divorced folk who will be reading this book. Let me repeat that the background of divorce is always sin. But, after all, all of us are sinners. Since God can forgive murderers, He can also forgive divorced folk. But we need to recognize that the root cause of divorce is sin.

Now our Lord is going to give something new—

> **And I say unto you, Whosoever shall put away his wife, except it be for fornication, and shall marry another, committeth adultery: and whoso marrieth her which is put away doth commit adultery [Matt. 19:9].**

Adultery breaks the marriage relationship and provides the *one* ground for divorce. Somebody says to me, "Yes, but here is this poor Christian woman, married to a drunkard!" Or a fine Christian man is married to a godless woman. What about that? Well, believers may *separate* on other grounds, which seems to be the whole point of 1 Corinthians 7, but divorce is permitted on only one basis, adultery.

Divorce was granted for the purpose of permitting the innocent party to remarry. This rule is applicable only to believers; God is not regulating the lives of unbelievers but is holding them to the message of the Cross first. God wants the unbeliever to come to Christ. He is lost whether he is married, divorced, or single. It makes no difference until he accepts Christ. The important thing to note is that for *believers* He puts down one ground for divorce: adultery.

Now suppose there is a believer whose spouse got a divorce on another ground. What about the innocent party? Well, if there has been adultery there, and in most cases there has been, then the innocent party is permitted to remarry. I believe that is the whole thought in this particular case.

Now, there is something else here that is important—

His disciples say unto him, If the case of the man be so with his wife, it is not good to marry [Matt. 19:10].

The disciples are saying, "Well, in that case it would be better to stay single." Well, you would avoid a lot of trouble—there is no question about that.

But he said unto them, All men cannot receive this saying, save they to whom it is given [Matt. 19:11].

This is so important, especially in our day. In the verse that follows, our Lord puts down a great principle. Even now the Roman Catholic church is wrestling with this problem.

For there are some eunuchs, which were so born from their mother's womb: and there are some eunuchs,

which were made eunuchs of men: and there be eunuchs, which have made themselves eunuchs for the kingdom of heaven's sake. He that is able to receive it, let him receive it [Matt. 19:12].

"There are some eunuchs, which were so born from their mother's womb." There are some men and some women who do not need to marry. They get along very well by themselves, but that's not for everybody.

"And there are some eunuchs, which were made eunuchs of men." Some churches make a rule that folk in certain positions are not to marry. They have no right to do that.

"And there be eunuchs, which have made themselves eunuchs for the kingdom of heaven's sake." I know a person who went to the mission field, and before she left, I talked to her. I said, "Look, your chances are nil for getting married out there." She said, "I have thought that through, and I am willing to make that sacrifice." She made it voluntarily.

Somebody says, "Do you think that the preacher ought to get married? Or do you think the priest should be married?" May I say to you, this is a place where God puts down a principle. He says that it is up to the individual. We have to make that decision for ourselves.

Now here is something wonderful—

JESUS RECEIVES LITTLE CHILDREN

Then were there brought unto him little children, that he should put his hands on them, and pray: and the disciples rebuked them.

But Jesus said, Suffer little children, and forbid them not, to come unto me: for of such is the kingdom of heaven.

And he laid his hands on them, and departed thence [Matt. 19:13–15].

This passage is ample basis for the salvation of children who die in infancy. It is a fact that no child will reject Jesus if He is presented to the child on a Bible basis. This is one reason why we should get the gospel message to them. Someone might say, "Wait a minute—then everyone could be saved if we reach them as children." No, this is not true because they reach the age of accountability later. The reason for trying to get the gospel into the hearts of children is so that when they reach the age of accountability they will make a decision for Christ. It is important that this be followed through. Do not rest on the fact that your child made a decision when he was two, three, four, five, six, seven or eight years old, etc. My daughter made a decision for Christ when she was seven. Ever since that time I have asked her many times if she has really trusted the Lord as Savior. One day she said, "Daddy, why do you keep asking me that question?" I told her I just wanted to make sure. Actually, the decision will be made at the age of accountability. You say to me, "When is that age?" I don't know. I just know that it is important to get the gospel to our children. Instead of standing on a street corner and arguing about it, let's get it to them and then follow through when they reach the age of accountability by doing everything in our power to get them to trust Christ.

It is interesting that our Lord, having spoken about the issue of divorce, immediately begins to talk about children. The children are all important in any divorce. A woman once came to me wanting a divorce because she no longer loved her husband. She said, "Because of all the things he is doing, I no longer love him, and I have heard you say that when there is no love, there is no relationship. So I want to get a divorce." It is true that when there is no love there is no relationship, and that is tragic, but that is not the basis for divorce. I said to this woman, "You tell me that you don't love your husband, but do you love your children?" She said, "Of course I do, but what has that got to do with it?" I told her that it has everything to do with it. "You are to stay with him as long as you can if you love those children." My friend, the fact that our Lord said, "Let the little children come unto Me," ought to make any couple, especially a Christian couple, make every effort to hold their marriage together. A large percentage of children and young folk who are in trouble with the law come from broken homes. You would be surprised to learn the number of little ones who have been turned away from Christ because of the divorced parents. It is very significant that Jesus ties together the subject of divorce and His loving concern for little children.

THE RICH YOUNG RULER

And, behold, one came and said unto him, Good Master, what good thing shall I do, that I may have eternal life?

And he said unto him, Why callest thou me good? there is none good but one, that is, God: but if thou wilt enter into life, keep the commandments [Matt. 19:16–17].

Notice how this young man approaches the Lord Jesus. He addresses Him as Good Master. He is willing to concede that He is good, and probably the enemies of Jesus would not have gone that far.

"Why callest thou me good?" I am sure you can see what our Lord was after. When He said, "There is none good but one, that is, God," He was saying in effect, "If you see that I am good, it is because I am God." He is directing his thinking so that he might accept Him as the Christ, the Son of God. Then the Lord Jesus flashed on this young man's life the commandments that have to do with a man's relationship to his fellowman.

He saith unto him, Which? Jesus said, Thou shalt do no murder, Thou shalt not commit adultery, Thou shalt not steal, Thou shalt not bear false witness,

Honour thy father and thy mother: and, Thou shalt love thy neighbour as thyself.

The young man saith unto him, All these things have I kept from my youth up: what lack I yet? [Matt. 19:18–20].

This young man could say that he had kept these commandments, and yet he recognized a lack in his life. The commandments which our Lord gave him compose the last section of the Decalogue which has to do with a man's relationship to man. The first of the Ten Commandments have to do with man's relationship to God. Our Lord did not use those because He was leading this young man along in his thinking. However, now the Lord directs his thinking to his relationship to God—

> **Jesus said unto him, If thou wilt be perfect, go and sell that thou hast, and give to the poor, and thou shalt have treasure in heaven: and come and follow me [Matt. 19:21].**

"If thou wilt be perfect," meaning *complete*. Following Jesus would have led him to see that he was not keeping the first commandments which have to do with a man's relationship to God. The Lord Jesus was on His way to the Cross. If this man followed Jesus, it would be to the foot of a cross. Something, however, was preventing him from going after the Lord. His riches were his stumbling block. For you and for me it might be something entirely different.

> **But when the young man heard that saying, he went away sorrowful: for he had great possessions [Matt. 19:22].**

It was his money that was keeping him from the Lord Jesus Christ. In our day there are many things that are keeping folk away from the Lord Jesus. Riches are only one thing; there are multitudes of other things. Actually, church membership is keeping many people from Christ because it puts them into a little cellophane bag that protects them from facing their sins. They feel secure because they have been through the ceremonies or have made their confession, and yet they may be as unconverted as any pagan in the darkest spot on topside of the earth. Today, is there something that is separating you from

Christ? Is there anything in the way that is keeping you from Him? Well, it was riches for this young man—

Then said Jesus unto his disciples, Verily I say unto you, That a rich man shall hardly enter into the kingdom of heaven [Matt. 19:23].

This is still true in our day—not many rich, not many noble, not many of the great ones of the earth are Christians.

And again I say unto you, It is easier for a camel to go through the eye of a needle, than for a rich man to enter into the kingdom of God [Matt. 19:24].

Many people miss the humor that our Lord sometimes used, and this passage is an example of it. There are some people who hold to the ridiculous explanation that there was a gate in Jerusalem called "The Eye of the Needle," that a camel had to kneel to pass through it, and that therefore the Lord was saying that a man had to become humble to enter the Kingdom of Heaven. Well, that misses the point altogether. Our Lord is talking about a real camel and a real needle with an eye. My friend, let me ask you a very plain question: Is it possible for a real camel to go through the eye of a real needle? I think you know the answer—he won't make it! It is impossible. But would it be possible for God to put a camel through a needle's eye? Well, God is not in that business, but He could do it. And only *God* can regenerate a man. That is the point our Lord is making here. It is easier for a camel to go through the eye of a needle than for a rich man to enter into the Kingdom of God.

Many people today think they are going to be saved by who they are or by what they have. You are truly saved when you find out that you are a sinner, a beggar in God's sight, with nothing to offer Him for your salvation. As long as a person feels he can *do* something or *pay* God for salvation, he can no more be saved than a camel can be put through the eye of a needle.

> **When his disciples heard it, they were exceedingly amazed, saying, Who then can be saved? [Matt. 19:25].**

Listen to Jesus' answer—

> **But Jesus beheld them, and said unto them, With men this is impossible; but with God all things are possible [Matt. 19:26].**

This is the explanation. As far as any person is concerned—regardless of who you are—you are a candidate for salvation if you recognize that you have nothing to offer God but come to Him like a beggar with empty hands. When you come to Him like that, He can save you. With *God* all things are possible.

JESUS REWARDS HIS APOSTLE

> **Then answered Peter and said unto him, Behold, we have forsaken all, and followed thee; what shall we have therefore? [Matt. 19:27].**

It is easy for us to think that Simon Peter is betraying a very selfish streak here. Did our Lord rebuke him?

> **And Jesus said unto them, Verily I say unto you, that ye which have followed me, in the regeneration when the Son of man shall sit in the throne of his glory, ye also shall sit upon twelve thrones, judging the twelve tribes of Israel [Matt. 19:28].**

Our Lord did not rebuke him. Instead, He told him what a great reward would be his. Likewise, I believe that today, we as Christians ought to be working for a reward.

> **And every one that hath forsaken houses, or brethren, or sisters, or father, or mother, or wife, or children, or**

lands, for my name's sake, shall receive an hundred-fold, and shall inherit everlasting life.

But many that are first shall be last; and the last shall be first [Matt. 19:29–30].

There is to be a reward for the saved ones who have sacrificed for Jesus' sake. Many an unknown saint, of whom the world has not heard, will be given first place in His presence someday. In that day I believe that many outstanding Christian leaders who receive wide acclaim in this life will be ignored while many unknown saints of God will be rewarded. What a glorious, wonderful picture this presents to us!

CHAPTER 20

THEME: Parable of the laborers in the vineyard; Jesus makes the fourth and fifth announcements of His approaching death, while the mother of James and John requests the places on the right and left for her sons; Jesus opens the eyes of two blind men along the roadside

This chapter opens with the parable of the laborers in the vineyard, which is a continuation, begun in the last chapter, of Jesus' remarks on rewards. This chapter brings to an end the section that seems to mark time in the movement in Matthew. From this chapter on, the tempo of Matthew increases, and the Lord moves directly to the Cross. This chapter also makes an important contribution to filling in some more of the dark corners of the present state of the Kingdom of Heaven. The principle for giving rewards is stated in this parable: Faithfulness to the task, rather than the amount of work done or the spectacular nature of the work, governs the giving of rewards.

PARABLE OF THE LABORERS IN THE VINEYARD

For the kingdom of heaven is like unto a man that is an householder, which went out early in the morning to hire labourers into his vineyard [Matt. 20:1].

This parable is closely related to the previous chapter. Matthew 19:30 says, "But many that are first shall be last; and the last shall be first." Verse 16 says, "So the last shall be first, and the first last: for many be called, but few chosen." So you see that at both the beginning and at the end of this parable the concept of the last being first and the first, last, forms sort of a parenthesis around it.

And when he had agreed with the labourers for a penny a day, he sent them into his vineyard.

And he went out about the third hour, and saw others standing idle in the marketplace,

And said unto them; Go ye also into the vineyard, and whatsoever is right I will give you. And they went their way.

Again he went out about the sixth and ninth hour, and did likewise [Matt. 20:2–5].

The "sixth" hour was high noon, and the "ninth" hour was three o'clock in the afternoon.

And about the eleventh hour he went out, and found others standing idle, and saith unto them, Why stand ye here all the day idle?

They say unto him, Because no man hath hired us. He saith unto them, Go ye also into the vineyard; and whatsoever is right, that shall ye receive.

So when even was come, the lord of the vineyard saith unto his steward, Call the labourers, and give them their hire, beginning from the last unto the first.

And when they came that were hired about the eleventh hour, they received every man a penny.

But when the first came, they supposed that they should have received more; and they likewise received every man a penny.

And when they had received it, they murmured against the goodman of the house,

Saying, These last have wrought but one hour, and thou hast made them equal unto us, which have borne the burden and heat of the day.

But he answered one of them, and said, Friend, I do thee no wrong: didst not thou agree with me for a penny?

> Take that thine is, and go thy way: I will give unto this
> last, even as unto thee.
>
> Is it not lawful for me to do what I will with mine own?
> Is thine eye evil, because I am good? [Matt. 20:6–15].

This is a tremendous parable which illustrates an important truth: It is not the amount of time which you serve nor the prominence or importance of your position which determines your reward. Rather, you will be rewarded for your faithfulness to the task which God has given you to perform, regardless of how small or how short or how insignificant it appears.

I have always felt that the Lord will someday reward a dear little lady who may have been a member of my church. I will turn to a member of my staff and say, "Do you know her?" He will say, "I have never heard of her. She did not sing in the choir, she was never president of any of our societies, and she never taught a Sunday school class. That woman didn't do anything, and look at the way the Lord is rewarding her!" We will probably find out that this dear lady was a widow with a young son. She never spoke to thousands of people like some evangelists and preachers, but she faithfully raised her one little boy, and he became a missionary who served God on a foreign field. The widow had been faithful in the task God had given her to do. Somebody might protest, "Well, she sure didn't work as hard as I did!" That might well be true, but God is not going to reward you for the *amount* of work you have done. He will reward you according to your faithfulness to the job which He called you to do. My friend, perhaps God has not called you to do something great for Him, but are you faithful in what He has assigned to you?

JESUS' FOURTH ANNOUNCEMENT OF HIS DEATH AND RESURRECTION

> And Jesus going up to Jerusalem took the twelve disciples apart in the way, and said unto them [Matt. 20:17].

Notice the physical and geographical movement of this section. Jesus and His disciples are going up out of the Jordan Valley and are approaching Jerusalem where He is to die upon the Cross.

> **Behold, we go up to Jerusalem: and the Son of man shall be betrayed unto the chief priests and unto the scribes, and they shall condemn him to death,**
>
> **And shall deliver him to the Gentiles to mock, and to scourge, and to crucify him: and the third day he shall rise again [Matt. 20:18–19].**

Our Lord couldn't spell it out any plainer than that. This is the fourth time He is telling them—in *detail* at this juncture—exactly what is going to happen to Him. Somehow or other the disciples didn't comprehend it—it just didn't fit into their program. However, as you and I read it now, we see very clearly that it was Christ's avowed intention to go to Jerusalem to die. Let's ponder the significance of this. He went there deliberately to die for you and for me. That is something to think about. The disciples of Jesus just couldn't believe it!

THE REQUEST OF THE MOTHER OF JAMES AND JOHN

At the time of Jesus' significant announcement of His pending death, the mother of James and John came to Jesus to ask Him a favor.

> **Then came to him the mother of Zebedee's children with her sons, worshipping him, and desiring a certain thing of him [Matt. 20:20].**

There are a great many of us who worship Him with the same motive!

> **And he said unto her, What wilt thou? She saith unto him, Grant that these my two sons may sit, the one on**

> **thy right hand, and the other on the left, in thy kingdom**
> **[Matt. 20:21].**

On any other occasion and at any other time, this request would be a
natural one for a mother who was ambitious for her children. In this
instance, however, she missed the atmosphere and the very understanding of what was really taking place at that time. The Lord will
answer her, and in quoting the following Scripture, I am going to
leave out a portion that is not in our better manuscripts.

> **But Jesus answered and said, Ye know not what ye ask.**
> **Are ye able to drink of the cup that I shall drink of? . . .**
> **They say unto him, We are able.**
>
> **And he saith unto them, Ye shall drink indeed of my**
> **cup, . . . but to sit on my right hand, and on my left, is**
> **not mine to give, but it shall be given to them for whom it**
> **is prepared of my Father [Matt. 20:22–23].**

When these two verses are read with omissions, the sense becomes
clear. My friend, don't miss the meaning here because it is so important to Christians today. Our Lord is not saying that there is no place at
His right hand and left hand for somebody. He is saying that He will
not *arbitrarily* give the positions to James and John or to anyone else.
Rather, the places are for those who prepare themselves for them.

Note this very carefully: Heaven is for the asking. You do nothing,
nothing, for salvation. You are saved by faith in Christ through His
marvelous grace. However, my friend, your position, your reward in
heaven is determined by what you do down here on earth. That is very
important, and Christians seem to have lost sight of it. What kind of a
place are you preparing for yourself? Personally, I have no ambition
for the places on Christ's right or left hand—I'm sure I have missed
those—but I *am* working for a place. All of us should be doing this. In
Philippians 3:14 Paul said, "I press toward the mark for the prize of
the high calling of God in Christ Jesus." The trouble with Christians
today is that too few are even trying to win anything. We need to rec-

ognize salvation as a free gift, but we need to get on the race course in order to receive a reward.

> **And when the ten heard it, they were moved with indignation against the two brethren [Matt. 20:24].**

Do you know why they were moved with indignation? It was because *they* wanted the places at His right and left hands!

> **But Jesus called them unto him, and said, Ye know that the princes of the Gentiles exercise dominion over them, and they that are great exercise authority upon them.**
>
> **But it shall not be so among you: but whosoever will be great among you, let him be your minister;**
>
> **And whosoever will be chief among you, let him be your servant [Matt. 20:25–27].**

This is a new approach to service and greatness, and it ought to be very clear in the minds of those who are engaged in Christian service. My friend, if you are going to sing for the Lord, please don't try to walk over all the other soloists. If you are trying to be a preacher of the gospel, don't try to push aside every other minister. If you are trying to be a church officer, don't do it at the expense of someone else. Our Lord makes it very clear that the way to be great and the way to serve Him is to take the lowest place.

Now, as Jesus and His disciples are very near to the city of Jerusalem, for the fifth time He tells them of His approaching death.

> **Even as the Son of man came not to be ministered unto, but to minister, and to give his life a ransom for many [Matt. 20:28].**

This is a tremendous verse, and every Christian ought to memorize it. This verse should be at your fingertips so that when an opportunity to witness comes, you will be able to tell just why Jesus Christ came into the world and what His mission was, because there is still confusion at that point.

JESUS HEALS TWO BLIND MEN

And as they departed from Jericho, a great multitude followed him [Matt. 20:29].

Jesus and His disciples are going from Jericho to Jerusalem, which is the opposite direction from the man who went down from Jerusalem to Jericho and fell among thieves. The Lord is going from Jericho up to Jerusalem to *die* with thieves. That's on the other side of the freeway, and on that side you and I can never go. We can only come to Him in faith, for He died in our stead.

By the way, some folk think that because at His trial He did not defend Himself, He never defended Himself, and that Christians should follow the same policy. However, at other times He did defend Himself. When He went to Jerusalem to die, He did not defend Himself because He was taking my place, and I'm guilty. Believe me, there was no defense! That is the reason He did not open His mouth at that time. He was bearing my sin, and He was bearing your sin at that time.

And, behold, two blind men sitting by the way side, when they heard that Jesus passed by, cried out, saying, Have mercy on us, O Lord, thou son of David [Matt. 20:30].

I love these two fellows—no one could keep them quiet!

And the multitude rebuked them, because they should hold their peace: but they cried the more, saying, Have mercy on us, O Lord, thou son of David [Matt. 20:31].

Notice that they addressed Him accurately—"O Lord, thou son of David." They acknowledged His kingship. The Syrophoenician at first called Him the son of David, but the Lord reminded her that she had no claim on Him in this way. These men, however, were Jews and did have a claim on Him, and they exercised their claim!

> **And Jesus stood still, and called them, and said, What will ye that I shall do unto you?**
>
> **They say unto him, Lord, that our eyes may be opened [Matt. 20:32–33].**

The problem of these men seemed so obvious. Why did the Lord ask what He could do for them? My friend, when you come to the Lord Jesus Christ, you must tell Him your need. If you are coming to Him for salvation, you must tell Him that you are a sinner and need His salvation. If you don't, you will not be saved. That's the offense of the Cross. Everybody would like to come to the Cross if they could bring along the perfume of their self-righteousness and good deeds. But, my friend, you and I haven't any goodness at all, none whatsoever, to present to God. You can no more sweeten human character with training and psychology and education than you can sweeten a pile of fertilizer out in the barnyard with Chanel No. 5. We have to come to Him as sinners and receive Him as our Savior. And the blind men came to the Lord Jesus with their need, "Lord, that our eyes may be opened"!

> **So Jesus had compassion on them, and touched their eyes: and immediately their eyes received sight, and they followed him [Matt. 20:34].**

Our Lord healed them, and they followed Him. Remember where He is going—He is on His way to the Cross.

CHAPTER 21

THEME: Jesus enters Jerusalem officially, cleanses the temple, curses the fig tree, and when He is challenged by the chief priests and elders, He condemns them by parables of the two sons and the householder whose servants slew his son

The movement in Matthew comes back into sharp focus in this chapter. Jesus comes to Jerusalem in a new role. Heretofore He had entered the city unobtrusively. Now He presses His claims as King upon the city of the King. Nothing could be more forward or daring. He cleanses the temple for the second time. This is presumption of the first order if He is not the One whom He claims to be. He curses the fig tree, which is a symbolic action. He meets the challenge of the religious rulers and by parable accuses them of plotting His death.

You will note the decisive and deliberate tone in the method of Jesus. He is forcing the issue now. He will force them to act when and how He chooses. He is in full control of the entire situation. He is never more kingly than when He approaches the Cross.

THE SO-CALLED TRIUMPHAL ENTRY

And when they drew nigh unto Jerusalem, and were come to Bethphage, unto the mount of Olives, then sent Jesus two disciples,

Saying unto them, Go into the village over against you, and straightway ye shall find an ass tied, and a colt with her: loose them, and bring them unto me.

And if any man say aught unto you, ye shall say, The Lord hath need of them; and straightway he will send them [Matt. 21:1–3].

I see no point in reading a miracle into this incident, although many people do. I believe this is a normal, natural situation. Probably when our Lord was in Jerusalem the last time He made arrangements with some friends to use these animals the next time He came to the city. He may have disclosed to them what He intended to do, and they agreed to have them ready for Him at the Passover Feast. I think that He told them that He would send a couple of His disciples to get them and that He would tell them what to say—"The Lord hath need of them." I feel that this incident is much more wonderful if we look at it in this way.

> **All this was done, that it might be fulfilled which was spoken by the prophet, saying,**
>
> **Tell ye the daughter of Sion, Behold, thy King cometh unto thee, meek, and sitting upon an ass, and a colt the foal of an ass [Matt. 21:4–5].**

This is a quotation from Zechariah 9:9—"Rejoice greatly, O daughter of Zion; shout, O daughter of Jerusalem: behold, thy King cometh unto thee: he is just, and having salvation; lowly, and riding upon an ass, and upon a colt the foal of an ass."

There are certain important omissions in the quotation in Matthew which a careful comparison will reveal. "Rejoice greatly, O daughter of Zion" is omitted. Why? Because our Lord is not coming into Jerusalem for that time of rejoicing. That will take place at His second coming. Also omitted is "he is just, and having salvation"—the word *salvation* has the thought of victory, which will be fulfilled at His second coming. The conclusion to be drawn from these portions is that at His second coming there will be a true triumphal entry.

It is assumed that our Lord was displaying His meekness by riding upon this little donkey. That is not true. This little animal was ridden by kings. In our day it would be like riding into town in a Rolls Royce. The donkey was the animal of peace while the horse was the animal of war. When Jesus came into Jerusalem riding on this little animal of peace, He was offering Himself as King. In spite of the fact that He was doing that, the prophet says that He was humble. That is very important to see.

> **And the disciples went, and did as Jesus commanded them,**
>
> **And brought the ass, and the colt, and put on them their clothes, and they set him thereon.**
>
> **And a very great multitude spread their garments in the way; others cut down branches from the trees, and strawed them in the way.**
>
> **And the multitudes that went before, and that followed, cried, saying, Hosanna to the son of David: Blessed is he that cometh in the name of the Lord; Hosanna in the highest [Matt. 21:6–9].**

It is possible that He had never come into Jerusalem by this route before—we'll see that in the Gospel of John. I think that generally He came in by the sheep gate in a very unobtrusive manner, the gate through which the animals for sacrifice were brought. But not this time! Here He rides in as a King, and those who are with Him recognize Him as a King. It is their opportunity to accept Him or reject Him.

> **And when he was come into Jerusalem, all the city was moved, saying, Who is this?**
>
> **And the multitude said, This is Jesus the prophet of Nazareth of Galilee [Matt. 21:10–11].**

Our Lord forces Jerusalem to consider His claims for one final moment.

THE SECOND CLEANSING OF THE TEMPLE

> **And Jesus went into the temple of God, and cast out all them that sold and bought in the temple, and overthrew**

the tables of the moneychangers, and the seats of them
that sold doves,

And said unto them, It is written, My house shall be
called the house of prayer; but ye have made it a den of
thieves [Matt. 21:12–13].

That is very strong language, is it not? Now let me call your attention
to certain facts regarding the so-called triumphal entry. First of all, I
do not think that "triumphal" entry is the proper name for it because,
as we have seen, only certain portions of Zechariah's prophecy were
fulfilled. Our Lord came into the city of Jerusalem in order that He
might be the *Savior*. He was making the final public presentation of
Himself to the people. When you consider the four Gospel records
together, they present a composite picture. The obvious conclusion is
that He did not enter the city on only one day but on three separate
days.

The first time was on Saturday, the Sabbath Day. There were no
money changers on that day, and He looked around and left, "And
Jesus entered into Jerusalem, and into the temple: and when he had
looked round about upon all things, and now the eventide was come,
he went out unto Bethany with the twelve" (Mark 11:11). He entered
as *Priest*.

The second day He entered Jerusalem was on Sunday, the first day
of the week. The money changers were there, and He cleansed the
temple (vv. 12–13). On this day He entered as *King*.

The third day He entered Jerusalem was on Monday, the second
day of the week. At that time He wept over Jerusalem, then entered the
temple and taught and healed (see Luke 19:41–44, 47–48). He entered
as a *Prophet* that day.

As we compare these three records in Matthew, Mark, and Luke, it
becomes apparent that they record three different entries, and I believe that our Lord entered Jerusalem on three consecutive days and in
three consecutive roles—as Priest, as King, as Prophet. And He re-
tired each day to Bethany. Apparently, He did not spend the night in
the city until He was arrested.

Remember that the so-called triumphal entry ended at the cross. But He will come the second time in *triumph*. The writer to the Hebrews puts this together in a wonderful way: "So Christ was once offered to bear the sins of many; and unto them that look for him shall he appear the second time without sin unto salvation" (Heb. 9:28). We are told in Zechariah 14:4 that when He comes the next time to this earth, His feet will stand on the Mount of Olives—that's where He will touch down. Then when He enters the city of Jerusalem, that will be the triumphal entry! I cannot call these three entries into Jerusalem triumphal entries because He is on His way to the Cross to die for your sin and my sin.

After the Lord cleansed the temple, many came to Him for help:

> **And the blind and the lame came to him in the temple; and he healed them [Matt. 21:14].**

Notice how Matthew emphasizes the fact that multitudes of folk were healed.

> **And when the chief priests and scribes saw the wonderful things that he did, and the children crying in the temple, and saying, Hosanna to the son of David; they were sore displeased [Matt. 21:15].**

They resented it.

> **And said unto him, Hearest thou what these say? And Jesus saith unto them, Yea; have ye never read, Out of the mouth of babes and sucklings thou hast perfected praise?**
>
> **And he left them, and went out of the city into Bethany; and he lodged there [Matt. 21:16–17].**

"And he left them" indicates His rejection of the religious leaders.

"And went out of the city into Bethany." As we have indicated, our Lord did not spend the night in Jerusalem until the night of His arrest.

But we find Him coming back into the city the next day. This, I think, is the entry that Luke emphasizes for us, His third and last entry on Monday morning—

THE SCORCHED FIG TREE

Now in the morning as he returned into the city, he hungered.

And when he saw a fig tree in the way, he came to it, and found nothing thereon, but leaves only, and said unto it, Let no fruit grow on thee henceforward for ever. And presently the fig tree withered away [Matt. 21:18–19].

There has been a great deal of difficulty in attempting to interpret the fig tree incident. I have heard all sorts of ideas about what the fig tree represents. The fig tree, I believe, is symbolic of Israel as in Matthew 24, as we shall see. At least we can say with confidence that when our Lord came into the world, there was no fruit evidenced by the nation of Israel. There were only the outward leaves of a ritualistic, lifeless religion. This the Lord condemned. The nation of Israel went through a religious form, but they had no power. They had turned what God had given them into a dead, lifeless ritual without vitality and virility which no longer was accomplishing God's purpose. And I am of the opinion that God will deal the same way with the organized church which has turned its back upon the person of Jesus Christ.

Again let me say that I feel His cursing of the fig tree is symbolic. Certainly He condemned the nation of Israel, and the nation suffered devastating judgment in A.D. 70.

And when the disciples saw it, they marvelled, saying, How soon is the fig tree withered away! [Matt. 21:20].

To them this was an amazing thing.

Jesus answered and said unto them, Verily I say unto you, If ye have faith, and doubt not, ye shall not only do

**this which is done to the fig tree, but also if ye shall say
unto this mountain, Be thou removed, and be thou cast
into the sea; it shall be done.**

**And all things, whatsoever ye shall ask in prayer, be-
lieving, ye shall receive [Matt. 21:21–22].**

Our Lord is giving them a lesson in prayer, that there should be *faith*
in prayer. They marvel that the fig tree was cursed, and He tells them
that their problem is that they do not have faith to believe that God can
move in such a miraculous way.

Frankly, I do not believe that our business is cursing fig trees or
removing literal mountains. For many years I have lived in Southern
California right along the foothills of the San Gabriel Mountains. To
me they are lovely. I have never grown tired of them. I always enjoy
looking at them, and there are never two days when they are alike. In
Psalm 121 the psalmist says, "I will (lit., "Shall I . . .?") lift up mine
eyes unto the hills, from whence cometh my help?" I don't think that
he was implying that his help came from the hills, because he added,
"My help cometh from the LORD, which made heaven and earth" (Ps.
121:1–2). Certainly, I do not look to those mountains for help, only for
enjoyment, and I have never wanted to move them. I feel that there is
something bigger and more important to do than mountain moving
and fig tree cursing. To preach the gospel of Christ, to give out the
Word of God so that the Spirit of God can use it—that, my friend, is a
miracle! When these lips of clay can say something that the Spirit of
God can use to transform a life, that involves the kind of faith that I
want. What we need is faith to believe that God can and will use His
Word.

THE SEARCHING QUESTION

Again Jesus is challenged by the religious authorities—

**And when he was come into the temple, the chief priests
and the elders of the people came unto him as he was**

teaching, and said, By what authority doest thou these things? and who gave thee this authority? [Matt. 21:23].

The religious rulers are becoming ugly and very hateful in their manner. They do not question what the Lord Jesus is doing. Do you notice that? They have no basis on which they can deny the miraculous things He does; they can only question His authority.

And Jesus answered and said unto them, I also will ask you one thing, which if ye tell me, I in like wise will tell you by what authority I do these things [Matt. 21:24].

Here is His question to them—

The baptism of John, whence was it? From heaven, or of men? And they reasoned with themselves, saying, If we shall say, From heaven; he will say unto us, Why did ye not then believe him?

But if we shall say, Of men; we fear the people; for all hold John as a prophet [Matt. 21:25–26].

You see, these religious rulers were attempting to trap Him by putting Him on the horns of a dilemma, but He immediately put them on the horns of a dilemma. He said, "I'll tell you by what authority I work if you will tell Me by what authority John the Baptist did his work. Was it from heaven or was it of men?" Of course, if they had said it was of heaven, our Lord would have said, "I move by the same authority." So they would not answer Him. They would not accept John's authority as being from heaven; so, of course, they would not accept Jesus' authority either.

And they answered Jesus, and said, We cannot tell. And he said unto them, Neither tell I you by what authority I do these things [Matt. 21:27].

You can sense the tension developing in this situation. The Lord is about to deliver a scathing denunciation of the religious rulers. He will give a parable that places publicans and harlots above them, and the charge of Jesus cannot be ignored. The Lord is moving against these two men.

PARABLE OF THE TWO SONS

But what think ye? A certain man had two sons; and he came to the first, and said, Son, go work to-day in my vineyard.

He answered and said, I will not; but afterward he repented, and went.

And he came to the second, and said likewise. And he answered and said, I go, sir: and went not.

Whether of them twain did the will of his father? They say unto him, The first. Jesus saith unto them, Verily I say unto you, That the publicans and the harlots go into the kingdom of God before you [Matt. 21:28–31].

This parable was a terrible insult to the religious rulers. Jesus likens them to the second son who said he would work for his father but did not. The Lord places publicans and harlots on a higher plane than these religious leaders.

This parable applies today. Many people have joined the church and are religious and think they are Christians, but they are not. They can perform their church rituals and give mental assent to the doctrines, but they are not genuine believers unless there has been a transformation in their lives. "Therefore if any man be in Christ, he is a new creature: old things are passed away; behold, all things are become new" (2 Cor. 5:17). The publicans and harlots recognized their sinfulness and came to Christ for salvation. They came late—at first they had said no to God, but they repented and came to Him, and He received them.

> For John came unto you in the way of righteousness, and
> ye believed him not: but the publicans and the harlots
> believed him: and ye, when ye had seen it, repented not
> afterward, that ye might believe him [Matt. 21:32].

The religious rulers had a religion of exterior decorations with nothing real inside. When a person accepts Jesus Christ as Savior, the interior is not only redecorated, it is made new.

Now our Lord gives them another parable before they can get out of earshot—

PABABLE OF THE HOUSEHOLDER AND HIS VINEYARD

In this parable the householder represents God the Father, and the son is the Lord Jesus Christ. The husbandmen are a picture of Israel.

> Hear another parable: There was a certain householder,
> which planted a vineyard, and hedged it round about,
> and digged a winepress in it, and built a tower, and let it
> out to husbandmen, and went into a far country:
>
> And when the time of the fruit drew near, he sent his
> servants to the husbandmen, that they might receive the
> fruits of it.
>
> And the husbandmen took his servants, and beat one,
> and killed another, and stoned another.
>
> Again, he sent other servants more than the first: and
> they did unto them likewise.
>
> But last of all he sent unto them his son, saying, They
> will reverence my son.
>
> But when the husbandmen saw the son, they said among
> themselves, This is the heir; come, let us kill him, and
> let us seize on his inheritance [Matt. 21:33–38].

This is the most pointed parable that our Lord has given so far. It is His final warning to the religious rulers. When in the parable He said, "But last of all he sent unto them his son," the Son was standing before them, giving them the parable. What are they going to do with God's Son? He is telling them right now what is in their hearts.

> **And they caught him, and cast him out of the vineyard, and slew him [Matt. 21:39].**

This was startling to these men!

> **When the lord therefore of the vineyard cometh, what will he do unto those husbandmen?**
>
> **They say unto him, He will miserably destroy those wicked men, and will let out his vineyard unto other husbandmen, which shall render him the fruits in their seasons [Matt. 21:40–41].**

Now He sends them back to the Old Testament for the analogy of the "stone" to Himself.

> **Jesus saith unto them, Did ye never read in the scriptures, The stone which the builders rejected, the same is become the head of the corner: this is the Lord's doing, and it is marvellous in our eyes?**
>
> **Therefore say I unto you, The kingdom of God shall be taken from you, and given to a nation bringing forth the fruits thereof [Matt. 21:42–43].**

It is interesting to note that the Lord changed the expression "kingdom of heaven" to "kingdom of God." I feel that He is using the larger term because He is getting ready to include the Gentiles and everybody that will come to Him.

"The kingdom of God shall be taken from you, and given to a nation bringing forth the fruits thereof"—that is, taken from the Jews and given to the church. "But ye are a chosen generation, a royal priesthood, an holy nation, a peculiar people; that ye should shew forth the praises of him who hath called you out of darkness into his marvellous light" (1 Pet. 2:9). The church is that "holy nation."

And whosoever shall fall on this stone shall be broken: but on whomsoever it shall fall, it will grind him to powder [Matt. 21:44].

"Whosoever shall fall on this stone shall be broken" relates to Christ's first coming. He is the Rock on which the church is built. "For other foundation can no man lay than that is laid, which is Jesus Christ" (1 Cor. 3:11). To fall on that Stone is to come to Christ for salvation in this day of grace. To reject Christ is to have the Stone fall later in the judgment about which Daniel prophesied (see Dan. 2:34, 44–45), which relates to Christ's second coming. And when the chief priests and Pharisees had heard his parables, they perceived that he spake of them [Matt. 21:45].They knew what He was talking about. In our day, unfortunately, a great many folk don't see that there is also an application for themselves, especially for those in the church.

But when they sought to lay hands on him, they feared the multitude, because they took him for a prophet [Matt. 21:46].

Although the religious rulers had determined that Jesus should die, when they attempted to seize Him, they became fearful of the multitudes who considered Him a prophet of God.

CHAPTER 22

THEME: *Jesus gives the parable of the marriage feast for the king's son; Jesus answers and silences the Herodians, the Sadducees, and the Pharisees*

Chapter 21 closed with the religious rulers determined that Jesus would die. "They sought to lay hands on him" (Matt. 21:46), but they were afraid of the multitude at that time. The chapter before us continues the verbal clash our Lord is having with the religious rulers. He gives them first the parable of the king who made a marriage feast. This is His continuing answer to the chief priests and elders which He began in the previous chapter.

PARABLE OF THE MARRIAGE FEAST

This is one of the greatest parables Jesus gave for the period in which you and I live.

> **And Jesus answered and spake unto them again by parables, and said [Matt. 22:1].**

Take note of the word *again*. This little word indicates that Jesus is still addressing the chief priests and elders mentioned in Matthew 21:23.

> **The kingdom of heaven is like unto a certain king, which made a marriage for his son [Matt. 22:2].**

Obviously, "a certain king" is God the Father, and "his son" is the Lord Jesus. Notice that He resorts to the expression "kingdom of heaven" instead of Kingdom of God which He used in the previous two parables. This parable parallels the Matthew 13 parables. But the emphasis here is upon how and why this age began rather than upon the conclusion of the age, which we saw in Matthew 13.

**And sent forth his servants to call them that were bidden
to the wedding: and they would not come [Matt. 22:3].**

He "sent forth his servants to call them that were bidden to the wedding." Who were bidden? The lost sheep of the house of Israel—our Lord had sent His apostles to them, you recall. And the prophets had been the messengers back in the Old Testament.

**Again, he sent forth other servants, saying, Tell them
which are bidden, Behold, I have prepared my dinner:
my oxen and my fatlings are killed, and all things are
ready: come unto the marriage [Matt. 22:4].**

What was the response?

**But they made light of it, and went their ways, one to his
farm, another to his merchandise:**

**And the remnant took his servants, and entreated them
spitefully, and slew them [Matt. 22:5–6].**

This was Israel's rejection of God's invitation. They killed His messengers, including the Lord Jesus Himself.

**But when the king heard thereof, he was wroth: and he
sent forth his armies, and destroyed those murderers,
and burned up their city [Matt. 22:7].**

This undoubtedly refers to the destruction of Jerusalem in A.D. 70 by Titus the Roman.

**Then saith he to his servants, The wedding is ready, but
they which were bidden were not worthy [Matt. 22:8].**

Now we will see a definite change in the method and manner of the invitation, and it refers to the present age in which we live—

> Go ye therefore into the highways, and as many as ye
> shall find, bid to the marriage.
>
> So those servants went out into the highways, and gath-
> ered together all as many as they found, both bad and
> good: and the wedding was furnished with guests
> [Matt. 22:9–10].

But notice what happens—

> And when the king came in to see the guests, he saw
> there a man which had not on a wedding garment [Matt.
> 22:11].

What is that wedding garment? The King's invitation is for everyone,
but there is a danger of coming without meeting the demands of the
King. That wedding garment is the righteousness of Christ which is
absolutely essential for salvation, and it is supplied to all who believe.
The apostle Paul speaks of this imputed righteousness: "But now the
righteousness of God without the law [that is, apart from the law] is
manifested, being witnessed by the law and the prophets; Even the
righteousness of [from] God which is by faith of Jesus Christ unto all
and upon all [it comes down upon all] them that believe: for there is
no difference" (Rom. 3:21–22). *All* have to have a wedding garment.

> And he saith unto him, Friend, how camest thou in
> hither not having a wedding garment? And he was
> speechless [Matt. 22:12].

Notice that he was speechless! I hear some folk say that they don't
need to receive Christ, that they will take their chances before God,
that they intend to argue their case. Well, our Lord said that this fellow without the wedding garment was *speechless.*

> Then said the king to the servants, Bind him hand and
> foot, and take him away, and cast him into outer dark-
> ness; there shall be weeping and gnashing of teeth.

For many are called, but few are chosen [Matt. 22:13–14].

Whether or not you accept the wedding garment is up to you, but Christ has provided it for you. The invitation has gone out to everyone, but you will have to come on the King's terms.

Now the enemies of Christ will make their final onslaught, their final attack upon the Lord Jesus. The Herodians will come first, the Sadducees will come next, and finally the Pharisees will come. Then our Lord will question the Pharisees—and they will try to get away from Him as quickly as they can. That marks the final break, and in chapter 23 we will hear Him denounce them.

The Herodians will come with the question of paying tribute to Caesar. The Sadducees will come with a question regarding the Resurrection. And the Pharisees will come with their question concerning the great commandment of the Law. We will see the marvelous way in which our Lord answers these men. May I say that I consider one of the proofs of His deity is the way in which He deals with the enemy.

JESUS ANSWERS THE HERODIANS

The Herodians come to Him with a question which is actually related to their particular position. They were a political party which favored the house of Herod and looked to those of that house to deliver them from the Roman yoke. I don't think the Herodians could be considered a religious party at all because they were strongly political. However, the Pharisees apparently used them, and it is quite possible that many of the Pharisees were Herodians as well.

Notice that the Pharisees instigate this first attack upon the Lord Jesus—

> **Then went the Pharisees, and took counsel how they might entangle him in his talk.**
>
> **And they sent out unto him their disciples with the Herodians, saying, Master, we know that thou art true,**

**and teachest the way of God in truth, neither carest thou
for any man: for thou regardest not the person of men.**

**Tell us therefore, What thinkest thou? Is it lawful to give
tribute unto Caesar, or not? [Matt. 22:15–17].**

Obviously, they were not wanting His opinion. They had their own
answer. It was a trick question. If He had said, "No, you are not to pay
tribute to Caesar," He could be accused of being a traitor to Rome, and
Rome was ruling over Israel at that time. If He had said, "Yes, you are
to pay tribute to Caesar," He could not be the true Messiah. They
thought that they had our Lord on the horns of a dilemma.

**But Jesus perceived their wickedness, and said, Why
tempt ye me, ye hypocrites? [Matt. 22:18].**

Notice that He called them what they were—hypocrites.

**Show me the tribute money. And they brought unto him
a penny [Matt. 22:19].**

It is notable that He used *their* coin. I have often wondered why He
didn't use His own coin. I think it is because He didn't have one.

**And he saith unto them, Whose is this image and super-
scription? [Matt. 22:20].**

They were using the legal tender of the Roman government, and here
it was a Roman coin.

**They say unto him, Caesar's. Then saith he unto them,
Render therefore unto Caesar the things which are Caesar's; and unto God the things that are God's [Matt.
22:21].**

This is an amazing answer because it involves more than just answering their question—and He certainly did that. In addition, He is say-

ing that they did owe something to Caesar. They were using his coins, they walked down Roman roads, and Rome did provide them with a measure of peace; so they did owe something to Rome. Therefore, render unto Caesar the things which are Caesar's. But there is another department: Render unto *God* the things that are *God's.*

When they had heard these words, they marvelled, and left him, and went their way [Matt. 22:22].

Obviously, this reveals that our Lord did not fall into their trap. Although they did owe Caesar something, that did not remove their responsibility to God.

The Herodians left Him, and now it's time for the Sadducees to come to bat, and they also attempt to trap Him—

JESUS ANSWERS THE SADDUCEES

The same day came to him the Sadducees, which say that there is no resurrection, and asked him,

Saying, Master, Moses said, If a man die, having no children, his brother shall marry his wife, and raise up seed unto his brother.

Now there were with us seven brethren: and the first, when he had married a wife, deceased, and, having no issue, left his wife unto his brother:

Likewise the second also, and the third, unto the seventh.

And last of all the woman died also. Therefore in the resurrection whose wife shall she be of the seven? for they all had her [Matt. 22:23–28].

The Sadducees did not believe in the Resurrection. They used a ridiculous illustration to try to trap the Lord. Imagine a woman who had had seven brothers for her husbands! She must have lived in Hollywood to accomplish this. Their question was, "Whose wife shall she be?" Now the Sadducees erred in two respects, and the Lord brings this to their attention.

Jesus answered and said unto them, Ye do ere, not knowing the scriptures, nor the power of God [Matt. 22:29].

The Sadducees were ignorant in two spheres: ignorant of the Scriptures and ignorant of the power of God. Ignorance of the Scriptures and ignorance of the power of God caused them to bring up such a ridiculous illustration. The explanation is simple—

For in the resurrection they neither marry, nor are given in marriage, but are as the angels of God in heaven [Matt. 22:30].

He is not saying that they are angels. Neither will we be angels in heaven. But we will be like angels in that we will not marry in heaven. In other words, in heaven there will not be any necessity to continue the race by means of birth. This does not mean that a husband and wife who were very close down here cannot be together in heaven. If they want to be together, of course they can be together. But, my friend, think of the ones who wouldn't want to be together. They won't have to be together. However, they both will have new dispositions, and probably they will get along lots better up there than they did down here!

But as touching the resurrection of the dead, have ye not read that which was spoken unto you by God, saying,

I am the God of Abraham, and the God of Isaac, and the God of Jacob? God is not the God of the dead, but of the living [Matt. 22:31–32].

This is a devastating statement! What about those who have gone before? What about Abraham today? Well, he is just as much Abraham today as he ever was. Abraham, Isaac, and Jacob have been simply transferred from earth to another place. They are not dead; they are alive. And this is true of your loved ones who are in Christ and are waiting in heaven for you. This is a glorious truth!

> **And when the multitude heard this, they were astonished at his doctrine [Matt. 22:33].**

JESUS ANSWERS THE PHARISEES

Now the Herodians and the Sadducees have been silenced. The Pharisees have been watching Jesus and these two groups. The Pharisees were a religio-political party. They wanted to see the kingdom of David brought back into power in order to rid themselves of Rome. In restoring the kingdom they could join the Herodians, but as a religious party they opposed the Sadducees. The Pharisees would correspond to the liberal wing of the church. The Pharisees, like the other two groups, were out to trap the Lord, and so their representative, a lawyer, posed a very interesting question.

> **But when the Pharisees had heard that he had put the Sadducees to silence, they were gathered together.**
>
> **Then one of them, which was a lawyer, asked him a question, tempting him, and saying [Matt. 22:34–35].**

The Pharisees have a huddle, then they plan a strategy and put forth this very clever lawyer, that is, a scribe, an expert in the Mosaic Law, to propound a question—

> **Master, which is the great commandment in the law? [Matt. 22:36].**

Listen to the answer of the Lord Jesus—

Jesus said unto him, Thou shalt love the Lord thy God with all thy heart, and with all thy soul, and with all thy mind.

This is the first and great commandment [Matt. 22:37–38].

Notice that He did not pick any one of the Ten Commandments. He gives them a second one—

And the second is like unto it, Thou shalt love thy neighbour as thyself [Matt. 22:39].

When you put this down on your life, you will recognize that you are coming short of the glory of God.

Our Lord is very straightforward with this man. He says, "You want to know which is the greatest commandment. To love God is the greatest commandment, and to love your neighbor is the next greatest."

On these two commandments hang all the law and the prophets [Matt. 22:40].

These two commandments actually summarized the entire Mosaic Law. The answer of Jesus was so obviously accurate that if the Pharisees had been honest, they would have said, "We have fallen short. We cannot be saved by the Law; we do need a Savior." And at that time the Lord Jesus, the Savior, was almost under the shadow of the Cross.

JESUS PUTS A QUESTION TO THE PHARISEES

The Pharisees huddle again to try to trap Him with another question, but He beats them to the punch and asks them a question—

While the Pharisees were gathered together, Jesus asked them,

Saying, What think ye of Christ? whose son is he? They say unto him, The son of David.

He saith unto them, How then doth David in spirit call him Lord, saying,

The LORD said unto my Lord, Sit thou on my right hand, till I make thine enemies thy footstool? [Matt. 22:41–44].

The Lord Jesus is quoting Psalm 110:1. How could David call his son his Lord? The Pharisees would have to say that the son would have to be supernaturally born for David to call him "my Lord."

If David then call him Lord, how is he his son? [Matt. 22:45].

This is the searching question which our Lord put to the Pharisees.

There are several implications in this question which are tremendous. Our Lord said that David wrote Psalm 110, that he wrote it by the Holy Spirit, and that he wrote it about the Messiah. "If David then call him Lord, how is he his son?" How could David call his son superior unless He was? The only logical answer to this question is the virgin birth. Jesus is David's son, but He is greater than David. A son of David cannot be greater than David unless there is something greater introduced into the line to make a greater son. The records of the supernatural birth of Jesus afford the only satisfactory answer. The Lord of David got into David's line, as stated in Luke's Gospel, "And the angel answered and said unto her, The Holy Ghost shall come upon thee, and the power of the Highest shall overshadow thee: therefore also that holy thing which shall be born of thee shall be called the Son of God" (Luke 1:35). He is greater than David because He is the Lord from heaven.

The Lord Jesus was forcing the Pharisees to face up to the real issue and to acknowledge Him as David's son and as David's Lord.

This ended the verbal clash with the religious rulers.

And no man was able to answer him a word, neither durst any man from that day forth ask him any more questions [Matt. 22:46].

They made no verbal attack upon Him after this. They had determined His death, and that is the thing toward which they are going to move. They see that they cannot answer Him. This is one of the great proofs of His deity.

CHAPTER 23

THEME: Jesus warns the multitude against the scribes and Pharisees; pronounces woes upon the scribes and Pharisees; weeps over Jerusalem

This chapter concludes the clash between the Lord Jesus and the religious rulers. He warns the multitudes about them and then denounces the religious rulers in unmistakable terms. No words that ever fell from the lips of our Lord were more scathing. It is a merciless condemnation. If you read this chapter carefully, it will blanch your own soul.

JESUS WARNS AGAINST THE SCRIBES AND PHARISEES

Jesus' public denunciation of the Pharisees took place at the temple, the stronghold of His enemies.

Then spake Jesus to the multitude, and to his disciples,

Saying, The scribes and the Pharisees sit in Moses' seat [Matt. 23:1–2].

These religious rulers were in the place of authority, and they controlled the Old Testament Scriptures. They usurped that which they had no right to usurp. They occupied very much the same position that church leaders occupy today. People looked to them for the interpretation of the truth.

All therefore whatsoever they bid you observe, that observe and do; but do not ye after their works: for they say, and do not [Matt. 23:3].

That is, do as the Scriptures teach, but don't follow the works of scribes and Pharisees because they are not following the Word of God.

Listen to His sad commentary upon the religious rulers—

> **For they bind heavy burdens and grievous to be borne, and lay them on men's shoulders; but they themselves will not move them with one of their fingers.**
>
> **But all their works they do for to be seen of men: they make broad their phylacteries, and enlarge the borders of their garments,**
>
> **And love the uppermost rooms at feasts, and the chief seats in the synagogues,**
>
> **And greetings in the markets, and to be called of men, Rabbi, Rabbi [Matt. 23:4–7].**

These men liked to have titles. These men liked to be recognized. They liked to wear certain religious garments and habits which set them apart from other people and drew attention to their high position. Our Lord is condemning all of this.

> **But be not ye called Rabbi: for one is your Master, even Christ; and all ye are brethren [Matt. 23:8].**

"Be not ye called Rabbi"—meaning teacher. And in the church certain respect and honor belongs to a pastor, but he is no different from anyone else. He is just one of your brothers.

> **And call no man your father upon the earth: for one is your Father, which is in heaven.**
>
> **Neither be ye called masters: for one is your Master, even Christ [Matt. 23:9–10].**

A "father" is a life-giver. To call a man a "father" in spiritual matters is to put him in the place of God as the one who gives spiritual life. This is blasphemous. Only God the Father gives life. A "master" is one in a position of authority. Christ is the One in the position of authority as the head of the church today.

> **But he that is greatest among you shall be your servant.**

> **And whosoever shall exalt himself shall be abased; and he that shall humble himself shall be exalted [Matt. 23:11–12].**

If you want to be the greatest, then become the servant of all.

WOES PRONOUNCED AGAINST THE SCRIBES AND PHARISEES

Here we see the gentle Jesus using the harshest language that is in the entire Word of God. No prophet of the Old Testament denounced sin as the Lord Jesus denounces it.

Here in Southern California this section was called to the attention of a liberal preacher. He didn't even know it was in the Bible—he had never read the Bible! In our day there is a misunderstanding of who the Lord Jesus really is. Liberalism gives the impression that all He ever talked about was love. One of the banners that was carried about in a protest march in Berkeley a number of years ago bore the slogan "Jesus Yes, Church No." A senator from Oregon made a great deal of that, maintaining that the church is giving the wrong impression, that this generation wants Jesus, but that they don't want the church as it is. Well, I agree that the church in general is giving the wrong impression, but the main problem is that they have really misunderstood who Jesus is. He is not the "lovechild" that the liberal thinks He is. Certainly it is true that He loves sinners and died for sinners, but also He is going to judge sinners. We need to have a correct perspective of Him. Therefore, He is the One who is misunderstood in our day.

The average conception of the Lord Jesus is not even biblical. For example, I asked a liberal preacher this: "Was the Jesus in whom you believe virgin born?"

He said, "No."

"Did He die on the cross for the sins of the world?"

"No."

"Did He rise bodily from the grave?"

"No!"

"Well, I'd like to know where *that* Jesus ever originated. There are no documents which give any information about *that* Jesus living in the first century. The only documents we have tell of One who was virgin born, who performed miracles, who died for the sins of the world, who rose from the dead, who ascended into heaven, and who is returning to this earth as the *Judge*."

My friend, *this* Jesus is not generally known today, and yet He is the only Jesus Christ who has ever lived. The other one is a figment of the imagination.

Listen to Him now as He pronounces woes upon the scribes and Pharisees. This is strong language.

> **But woe unto you, scribes and Pharisees, hypocrites! for ye shut up the kingdom of heaven against men: for ye neither go in yourselves, neither suffer ye them that are entering to go in [Matt. 23:13].**

The Lord uses the term *woe* eight times in this section and calls scribes and Pharisees hypocrites seven times. He accuses them of blocking the way to heaven by their false leadership.

> **Woe unto you, scribes and Pharisees, hypocrites! for ye devour widows' houses, and for a pretence make long prayer: therefore ye shall receive the greater damnation [Matt. 23:14].**

In other words, these men made long prayers, but they were heartless and crooked in their business dealings.

> **Woe unto you, scribes and Pharisees, hypocrites! for ye compass sea and land to make one proselyte, and when**

> he is made, ye make him twofold more the child of hell
> than yourselves [Matt. 23:15].

Oh, they were great at going out and witnessing, but they were not bringing anyone to God. None of their converts were actually born again.

> Woe unto you, ye blind guides, which say, Whosoever
> shall swear by the temple, it is nothing; but whosoever
> shall swear by the gold of the temple, he is a debtor!
> [Matt. 23:16].

"He is a debtor!"—that is, his oath is binding.

> Ye fools and blind: for whether is greater, the gold, or
> the temple that sanctifieth the gold?

> And, Whosoever shall swear by the altar, it is nothing;
> but whosoever sweareth by the gift that is upon it, he is
> guilty [Matt. 23:17–18].

That is, he is guilty if he fails to carry out his oath.

> Ye fools and blind: for whether is greater, the gift, or the
> altar that sanctifieth the gift?

> Whoso therefore shall swear by the altar, sweareth by it,
> and by all things thereon.

> And, whoso shall swear by the temple, sweareth by it,
> and by him that dwelleth therein.

> And he that shall swear by heaven, sweareth by the
> throne of God, and by him that sitteth thereon [Matt.
> 23:19–22].

The Pharisees were teaching that if you swore by the temple or the altar, you were not bound to keep your oath. But if you swore by the *gold* of the temple or by the *gift* on the altar, the oath was binding. They were splitting hairs, of course, and they were placing the emphasis on material things rather than upon the spiritual purpose for which they were to be used.

Now listen to our Lord's strong denunciation—

Woe unto you, scribes and Pharisees, hypocrites! for ye pay tithe of mint and anise and cummin, and have omitted the weightier matters of the law, judgment, mercy, and faith: these ought ye to have done, and not to leave the other undone [Matt. 23:23].

They were very meticulous in tithing their little plants which produce condiments like mint, anise, and cummin. For instance, when I was a boy, my mother always grew a little patch of mint out in the backyard to put in iced tea in the summertime. Can you imagine one of these religious rulers measuring off a little patch of mint and taking a tenth of it to give to the Lord? Oh, they were so strict about those little matters! But our Lord says, "You have forgotten about the weightier matters of the law." And those weightier matters would have brought these men to the person of Christ.

Ye blind guides, which strain at a gnat, and swallow a camel [Matt. 23:24].

Do you think this verse is humorous? I do, and if I had been present when Jesus said this, I would have laughed—unless, of course, I had been a Pharisee or a scribe. The Lord said this in a serious vein, but I am sure many in the crowd laughed, especially those who knew the old religious rulers.

There are a lot of folk who make so much of little things. I remember a dear lady who used to argue about the use of lipstick. She thought it was awful, and yet she had the meanest tongue of any person I know. She didn't think that was bad, but lipstick was terrible. Frankly, the paint of gossip on the end of the tongue—especially when it is used to blacken somebody's reputation—is lots worse than a little paint on the lips. It is amazing how people can strain at a gnat and swallow a camel!

> **Woe unto you, scribes and Pharisees, hypocrites! for ye make clean the outside of the cup and of the platter, but within they are full of extortion and excess [Matt. 23:25].**

This fifth woe pictures the Pharisees with their emphasis on the externals. This is a picture of the average church today that is so busy making the outside of the cup and platter clean. They go through all the ceremonies. They want to have the best equipment. They talk so nice and piously on the outside, but inside they do not deal with sin. In most cases, they do not even like the word sin. But all of the external ceremonies cannot clean up their inner corruption. The Pharisees substituted ritual for reality, formality for faith, and liturgy for God.

> **Thou blind Pharisee, cleanse first that which is within the cup and platter, that the outside of them may be clean also [Matt. 23:26].**

Don't misunderstand Him. He is not saying that the outside should not be clean. But you give a wrong impression when the inside is dirty and the outside is not. The place to start is on the inside.

> **Woe unto you, scribes and Pharisees, hypocrites! for ye are like unto whited sepulchres, which indeed appear beautiful outward, but are within full of dead men's bones, and of all uncleanness [Matt. 23:27].**

To me this is the most frightening figure of speech which our Lord used. As I said previously, the cup and platter (saucer), clean on the outside and dirty on the inside, picture the average church in our day. But I am afraid that this simile of the tomb pictures the average church-goer—beautiful on the outside, but on the inside they are dead in trespasses and sins. They have a form of godliness, but they deny the power of it to make them new creations in Christ. My friend, until that happens to you, your church membership is null and void; it is nothing but hypocrisy. When I read that over half the population of the United States are church members, I wonder why in public places I see ninety-nine percent of the crowd drinking cocktails, using profanity, and telling dirty stories. We have a whole lot of marble tombs walking around, spiritual zombies, dead in trespasses and sins.

Even so ye also outwardly appear righteous unto men, but within ye are full of hypocrisy and iniquity [Matt. 23:28].

Oh, how He is denouncing religious leaders! And they *should* be denounced above everyone else. My friend, if you have a Bible-teaching church in your community and a preacher who believes the Book and is trying to teach it, for God's sake stand with him in these days. He needs you, and you need him. Oh, how we need men who believe the Word of God—and live it!

Woe unto you, scribes and Pharisees, hypocrites! because ye build the tombs of the prophets, and garnish the sepulchres of the righteous,

And say, If we had been in the days of our fathers, we would not have been partakers with them in the blood of the prophets.

Wherefore ye be witnesses unto yourselves, that ye are the children of them which killed the prophets.

Fill ye up then the measure of your fathers [Matt. 23:29–32].

And we are doing the same thing in our day. Great men of God, preachers, evangelists, missionaries, were denounced and ridiculed by their generations, but they are honored today. That was true of Spurgeon, Moody, Torrey, and many others. Our Lord sure did know human nature, and it has not changed. "You build the tombs to commemorate the prophets after they are gone, and you decorate the graves of the righteous!"

"Fill ye up then the measure of your fathers." These same religious leaders, who were honoring the prophets of the past, would soon force Rome to crucify the Son of God who was speaking to them.

Now this is something that will blanch your soul—

Ye serpents, ye generation of vipers, how can ye escape the damnation of hell? [Matt. 23:33].

Can you imagine stronger language than that? What does He mean by calling them a generation of vipers? He means that they are the off-spring of snakes! This is devastating to that damnable doctrine of the universal brotherhood of man and the universal Fatherhood of God. God does not claim you if you have rejected Jesus Christ. The *only* way to become a child of God is to receive Christ. "But as many as received him, to them gave he power [the right] to become the sons of God, even to them that believe on his name" (John 1:12).

The Lord is speaking in harsh terms in these verses in Matthew. He is serving a cup of tea that is a little too strong for a great many of the liberal-minded folk of this present hour. Jesus Christ was no love child. He came to earth to die for your sins because He loved you, but if you reject Him, He becomes your Judge.

Wherefore, behold, I send unto you prophets, and wise men, and scribes: and some of them ye shall kill and crucify; and some of them shall ye scourge in your syna-gogues, and persecute them from city to city:

That upon you may come all the righteous blood shed upon the earth, from the blood of righteous Abel unto the blood of Zacharias son of Barachias, whom ye slew between the temple and the altar [Matt. 23:34–35].

Apparently the slaying of Zacharias was an incident which had taken place recently. Our Lord starts at the beginning with the murder of Abel and brings them down to the present hour. He makes it very clear that God will judge Israel for destroying the righteous. He is certainly contradicting our current philosophy that everyone will ultimately be saved. He says that they will not be saved.

> **Verily I say unto you, All these things shall come upon this generation [Matt. 23:36].**

He is predicting the destruction of Jerusalem in A.D. 70. What does He do next? The One who made this strong denunciation will now *weep* over Jerusalem.

JESUS WEEPS OVER JERUSALEM

> **O Jerusalem, Jerusalem, thou that killest the prophets, and stonest them which are sent unto thee, how often would I have gathered thy children together, even as a hen gathereth her chickens under her wings, and ye would not!**
>
> **Behold, your house is left unto you desolate [Matt. 23:37–38].**

Jerusalem rejected Him in His so-called triumphal entry, and He has rejected Jerusalem, but now He weeps over this city. Yes, He denounced them, but He does love them. And knowing the judgment which must come, He weeps.

The statement was made in Dwight L. Moody's day that he was the only man living who should preach on hell because he did it with such compassion. And certainly our Lord pronounced these woes with a heart that was breaking. You remember that some of the people thought he was Jeremiah because, although Jeremiah gave the strongest denunciation in the Old Testament, he wept over it. I am of the opinion that we today should not make denunciations unless we are personally moved by them.

For I say unto you, Ye shall not see me henceforth, till ye shall say, Blessed is he that cometh in the name of the Lord [Matt. 23:39].

Not only were the religious rulers in shock, but His apostles were in shock, also. This seemed to them a strange turn of events. They expected Him to establish the Kingdom, with Jerusalem as the capital. But now He says that their house is to be left desolate and that they will not see Him again until they say, "Blessed is he that cometh in the name of the Lord." You see, although He is on His way to the Cross at this time, He gives them the assurance that He will return—and that will be His triumphal entry!

Obviously, the Kingdom is going to be postponed. There are many who object to that teaching, but to do that, they must object to the language of our Lord. He tells His disciples that He will not establish the kingdom on earth at this time but that He will come again to establish it. That means that the Kingdom is postponed, doesn't it? The apostles were surprised and disappointed at the idea of a postponement; so they come to Him with three questions, which we will see in the following chapter.

CHAPTER 24

THEME: The disciples ask Jesus three questions; He answers two about the sign of the end of the age and the sign of His coming

Matthew 24 and 25, known as the Olivet Discourse, constitute the last of three major discourses in this Gospel. They are called major discourses because of the extent, content, and intent of them.

JESUS PREDICTS THE DESTRUCTION OF JERUSALEM

Our Lord has now denounced the religious rulers. He has turned His back on Jerusalem and has told them that their house (temple) is left desolate.

And Jesus went out, and departed from the temple: and his disciples came to him for to shew him the buildings of the temple [Matt. 24:1].

The Lord Jesus has told them that His Kingdom would be postponed and that the temple would be left desolate. (The temple was made up of many buildings. This was the temple that Herod was having built, and the construction was still in progress. It was made of white marble, and at this time it was very large and very beautiful.) The disciples are disturbed at the statement of Jesus that it is to be left desolate. So the disciples come to Him, wanting to show Him around the buildings.

And Jesus said unto them, See ye not all these things? verily I say unto you, There shall not be left here one stone upon another, that shall not be thrown down [Matt. 24:2].

"See ye not all these things?" The disciples thought they saw it, and they ask Him to take a look. So He says to them, "Do you really *see* it?" In our contemporary society this is a good question for us to consider. Do we really *see* the world around us?

When my wife and I first came to Southern California, we spent every Monday, which was my day off, riding around looking at this fantastic place. (And it *was* fantastic in those days before everybody in the world tried to settle here!) After we had marveled at one beautiful spot after another, I would say to my wife, "But we really don't see it as it is. All of this is under God's judgment. It all will pass away." My friend, all these cultural centers, these great schools, these skyscrapers, these great cities which we see are going to pass away someday. It doesn't seem possible, and that is how the disciples felt.

Jesus continued by saying, "There shall not be left here one stone upon another, that shall not be thrown down." If His first statement put them in shock, this must have traumatized them.

When I was at the Wailing Wall in Jerusalem several years ago, the tour director tried to call my attention to the way the stones had been worn away by the people who had come there over the years to weep. That was certainly worth noting, but the thing that impressed me was that the wall was constructed of many kinds of stones. History tells us that the Wailing Wall was made up of stones which came from different buildings in different periods. At the pinnacle of the temple, which evidently was the corner of the temple area, recent excavations reveal the same thing—there are all kinds of stones from different periods. What does that mean? My friend, that means that not one stone was left upon another—the builders had to go and pick up stones from different places because in A.D. 70 Titus the Roman really destroyed that city!

Although this is ancient history to us, it was a shocking revelation to the disciples. They talked it over, I am sure, then came to Him with three questions.

And as he sat upon the mount of Olives, the disciples came unto him privately, saying, Tell us, when shall these things be? and what shall be the sign of thy coming, and of the end of the world? [Matt. 24:3].

(1) "When shall these things be?"—when one stone would not be left upon another; (2) "What shall be the sign of thy coming?"—The answer to this question is found in verses 23–51; and (3) "What shall be the sign . . . of the end of the world [completion of the age]?" The answer to this question is found in verses 9–22. The Lord Jesus is going to answer these three questions, and we call His answers the Olivet Discourse because it took place on the Mount of Olives.

JESUS ANSWERS THE DISCIPLES' QUESTIONS

The first question, "When shall these things be?"—when one stone shall not be left upon another—is not answered in the Gospel of Matthew. We find it in the Gospel of Luke, and we find segments of it in the Gospel of Mark. Why is it not included in Matthew's Gospel? Because Matthew is the Gospel of the Kingdom; it presents the King. The destruction of Jerusalem in A.D. 70 has something to do with this age in which we live, but it has nothing to do with the distant future when the King is coming. Therefore, Matthew does not carry that part of the Olivet Discourse.

Let's look at our Lord's answer to the first question, as recorded in Luke's Gospel: "And when ye shall see Jerusalem compassed with armies, then know that the desolation thereof is nigh. Then let them which are in Judaea flee to the mountains; and let them which are in the midst of it depart out; and let not them that are in the countries enter thereinto. For these be the days of vengeance, that all things which are written may be fulfilled. But woe unto them that are with child, and to them that give suck, in those days! for there shall be great distress in the land, and wrath upon this people. And they shall fall by the edge of the sword, and shall be led away captive into all nations: and Jerusalem shall be trodden down of the Gentiles, until the times of the Gentiles be fulfilled" (Luke 21:20–24).

Undoubtedly, many of those who heard the Lord Jesus say these things were present in A.D. 70 when the Roman armies surrounded the city, laid siege to it, cut it off from the rest of the world, then finally breached the wall and got in. What the Romans did was terrible. They demolished the city. It was the worst destruction in its history, more devastating than that conducted by Nebuchadnezzar over six centuries earlier. When the Romans destroyed Jerusalem in A.D. 70, the first part of the Olivet Discourse was fulfilled.

The next two questions asked by the disciples were these: "What shall be the sign of thy coming, and of the end of the world [age]?"

The Lord is going to answer the disciples' questions in their chronological and logical order. He will answer their last question first and their second question last. The first thing the Lord deals with is the sign of the end of the world, or more accurately, the end of the age. The world will never come to an end. The old world will pass away and a new earth will be brought on the scene. It will be similar to trading in your old car for a new one. You don't say "This is the end of the car-age for me. I don't have a car anymore." You do have a car because you traded your old one in and got a new one. And the Lord is going to trade the old world in for a new one. The world will never come to an end. But it will be the end of an age, and that is the word the disciples are using in their question to the Lord Jesus.

In this Olivet Discourse, when Christ speaks of His coming, He is referring to His return to the earth to establish His Kingdom. The church is not in the picture at all. In fact, by the end of the age, the church will have been removed, and it will be the last days of the nation Israel. He is speaking about the Great Tribulation period and so labels it in this discourse.

JESUS TRACES THE CHARACTERISTICS
OF THIS AGE

And Jesus answered and said unto them, Take heed that no man deceive you [Matt. 24:4].

The phrase "Take heed that no man deceive you" is characteristic of this entire age. The Lord gives this word of caution because there will be much deception, especially during the Tribulation period when the Antichrist will appear. Peter warns us in 2 Peter 2:1, "But there were false prophets also among the people, even as there shall be false teachers among you, who privily shall bring in damnable heresies, even denying the Lord that bought them, and bring upon themselves swift destruction." We don't have to worry about false prophets, because if anybody starts prophesying in our day, we Christians can pooh-pooh him right off the scene because prophets are not for this period. However, we are to beware of false teachers, and there are a great many of those around. We must test them by Scripture. In this morning's mail a letter has come to me which illustrates this fact. It has come from a woman who apparently has an important position in an insurance company. She tells of a well-meaning friend who introduced her to a cult. After going to her friend's church for one year, she heard our Bible-teaching radio program, and the Scripture alerted her to the error of the cult. Then she tells of how she and her entire family went to a good church in her area. My friend, we need to beware of false teaching. There is a lot of it around in our day. Our Lord warns, "Take heed that no man deceive you."

For many shall come in my name, saying, I am Christ; and shall deceive many [Matt. 24:5].

Near the end of the age many people will claim to be Christ. We have such people present with us now. One man established a "holy city" in Northern California and expected any minute to be called to Washington, D.C., to solve the problems of the world. There are no "holy cities" on the face of the earth, but someday the Lord will come from the Holy of Holies in heaven to earth and solve the problems. It should be remembered that even now there are many antichrists, but at the end of the age there will come one Antichrist who will oppose Christ and set himself up as the only authority.

I believe that our Lord, up there on the Mount of Olives, looked down to the end of the age and to the Great Tribulation period, but that at the beginning of His discourse, He bridged the gap by giving us a picture of the present age of the church. I recognize that there are many good Bible teachers, much better than I am, who take the position that in verses 5–8 He is speaking of the Tribulation period, also; so if you want to disagree with me, you will be in very good company.

However, it is my view that our Lord is not referring to the Great Tribulation until we reach verse 9 of this chapter.

And ye shall hear of wars and rumours of wars: see that ye be not troubled: for all these things must come to pass, but the end is not yet [Matt. 24:6].

Wars and rumors of wars are not the sign that we are at the end of the age, by any means. The Lord is bridging the gap from where the disciples are to the end of the age. It is easy to think of major wars as indicative of the fact that we are at the end of the age. They are not! There have been many major wars in the past few thousand years and only about two hundred years of peace. When I was a little boy at the end of World War I, I remember hearing my dad and others talking about the books being printed declaring it was the end of the world. World War I caused this type of thinking. But after the war, we had a worldwide depression, World War II, and the atom bomb. By this time, I was a pastor in Pasadena, and I told my congregation that a wheelbarrow load of books would come out saying that we were at the end of the world because of World War II. You know something? I was wrong! Two wheelbarrow loads of books were printed, and they were sensational.

We have come a long way from World War II, and the end of the age still has not come. We should listen to the Lord and stop listening to false teachers. We will hear about wars and rumors of wars, but we should not be troubled because all these things will come to pass, and still it will not be the end of the age. Friend, we should also keep in mind that man will never solve the problem of war. The League of Nations could not solve this problem, and the United Nations will not be able to solve it either. There will be no peace until the Prince of Peace comes.

For nation shall rise against nation, and kingdom against kingdom: and there shall be famines, and pestilences, and earthquakes, in divers places.

All these are the beginning of sorrows [Matt. 24:7–8].

These are characteristics of the entire age and are therefore not signs of the end of the age, "but the end is not yet" (v. 6). False christs, rumors of wars, famines, pestilences, and earthquakes characterize the entire church age, but they will apparently be intensified as we draw near to the end of the age. Right now the population explosion has the world frightened and rightly so. People are starving to death by the thousands and the millions. And this situation is going to increase. The old black horse of famine (see Rev. 6:5–6) hasn't appeared yet, but at the end of the age the black horse and its rider will come forth. What we see today is just the beginning of sorrows.

The next verse begins with our first time word:

THE BEGINNING OF THE TRIBULATION
WITH ITS SIGNS

Now the Lord begins to speak of the time of tribulation. You and I are living in the "age of the church" or the "age of the Holy Spirit," as some people like to speak of it. The Bible divides the world today into three groups of people: the Jews, the Gentiles, and the church of God (see 1 Cor. 10:32). In this age God is calling out a people to His name from both Jews and Gentiles to compose the third group, the church. It is this third group which will be taken out of the world at the time of the Rapture. Then the Great Tribulation will begin, and I believe that verse 9 speaks of this beginning—

Then shall they deliver you up to be afflicted, and shall kill you: and ye shall be hated of all nations for my name's sake [Matt. 24:9].

"Then shall they deliver you up to be afflicted"—who is the *you?* Obviously, He is not addressing the church but the nation Israel. The affliction He is talking about is anti-Semitism on a worldwide scale.

At this point let me inject an important fact for Christians in our day. As long as the true church is in the world, there could not be worldwide anti-Semitism because the church would resist it. No genuine believer in the Lord Jesus could hate the Jews; it is an impossibility. It is my feeling that the liberal wing of the church is presenting a false front to the Jews and that in the final analysis it will turn against them. But as long as the true church is in the world, there won't be worldwide anti-Semitism; it will break out *after* the church has been removed at the Rapture.

> **And then shall many be offended, and shall betray one another, and shall hate one another.**
>
> **And many false prophets shall rise, and shall deceive many [Matt. 24:10–11].**

As we saw earlier, the church is warned against false teachers while Israel is warned against false prophets. So here, after the church has been removed, again the warning is against false prophets.

> **And because iniquity shall abound, the love of many shall wax cold [Matt. 24:12].**

This is a *principle*, and there are many principles in this Olivet Discourse which we can apply to our own day. Not long ago I met a preacher who had been a schoolmate of mine. He has become liberal in his theology; he drinks his cocktails, smokes his cigarettes, and lives just like the rest of the world lives. He told me, "McGee, you don't fight city hall; you join it!" He told me about how sinful practices had gotten into his church and how he is not planning to fight them. When iniquity abounds, the love of many grows cold, and this will be even more true at the end of the age.

This next verse is very startling to some folk—

> **But he that shall endure unto the end, the same shall be saved [Matt. 24:13].**

The question is: Who endures to the end? Well, when I study the Book of Revelation, I find that God will stop all the forces of nature and of evil and even the forces of good while He seals a certain number of folk. So who is going to endure to the end? Those whom He seals at the beginning, of course. The Good Shepherd—in all ages—will bring His sheep through to the end. When He starts with a hundred sheep, He comes through with a hundred sheep.

When someone says to me, "So-and-so was very active in the church and has gone into sin. Is he saved?" I can only reply that I do not know. We will have to wait to see what happens. I tell people that the pigs will eventually end up in the pigpen, and the prodigal sons will all find their way back to the Father's house. It *is* confusing to find a son in a pigpen and a pig in the Father's house. Peter says, " . . . the sow that was washed [has returned] to her wallowing in the mire" (2 Pet. 2:22). Let's say that one of the little pigs went with the prodigal son to the father's house, that he was scrubbed clean, his teeth brushed with Pepsodent, and that a pink ribbon was tied around his neck. But he wouldn't stay in the father's house. Sooner or later he would go back to the pigpen where he belonged. "He that shall endure unto the end, the same shall be saved." You'll just have to wait and see. Sometimes a son, a Christian, will get into a pigpen, but since he is a son, he will get out someday. Why? Because he has a wonderful Shepherd. "The same shall be saved."

> **And this gospel of the kingdom shall be preached in all the world for a witness unto all nations; and then shall the end come [Matt. 24:14].**

The gospel of the Kingdom is what John the Baptist preached— "Repent ye: for the kingdom of heaven is at hand" (Matt. 3:2). And the Lord Jesus began His ministry with that message— "From that time Jesus began to preach, and to say, Repent: for the kingdom of heaven is at hand" (Matt.4:17). Also, He sent His apostles out with that message (see Matt. 10). But in Matthew 11:28, we saw that our Lord's message changed to "Come unto me, all ye that labour and are heavy laden, and I will give you rest." And in Matthew 20:28 He said that He had come to give His life a ransom for many. But during the Tribulation period the gospel of the Kingdom will again be preached. It is not for our day, because we are to preach the gospel of the grace of God. Is the gospel of the Kingdom another gospel? No, my friend, it is not. It is the same gospel with a different emphasis. We have no right to say that the Kingdom of Heaven is at hand because we don't know. But when the Great Tribulation period begins, the people will know that they are close to the end, although they will not know the day nor the hour. Therefore, the message will be, "Repent: for the kingdom of heaven is at hand."

Now let me answer our critics who say that we who hold the dispensational view of Scripture teach that there are two or more ways of being saved. No, God has never had more than one basis on which He saves men, and that basis is the Cross of Christ. Every offering before Christ came looked forward to the Cross of Christ, and every commemoration since He has come looks back to the Cross of Christ.

To illustrate this, let's go back to Genesis 4 and look at the offering which Abel brought to God. He brought a little lamb. If you had been there, you could have asked Abel, "Why are you bringing this little lamb? Do you think that a little lamb will take away your sins?" He would have said, "Of course not! I'm bringing this little lamb because God told me to do so. I am bringing it by faith." Then you could have asked him, "Well, if it won't take away your sins, why would He ask you to bring it?" Abel's answer would have been something like this: "This little lamb is pointing to One who is coming later, the seed of the woman, my mother. That One will take away our sins. I bring this little lamb by faith, recognizing that I am a sinner and need a substitute." You see, Abel was looking forward to the One who was coming.

John the Baptist not only said, "Repent ye: for the kingdom of heaven is at hand" (Matt. 3:2), but he also said, " . . . Behold the Lamb of God, which taketh away the sin of the world" (John 1:29). John identified Him. Before the coming of Christ everyone who had come to God on *His* terms was saved on *credit*. And they were forgiven on the basis of the death of Christ. In the Old Testament God never saved anyone by Law. At the heart of the Mosaic system was the sacrificial system. They brought a lamb to God because the Law revealed that they were lawbreakers, that they were not obeying God, and that they did need to have a substitute to pay the penalty of their sins. The Law was given " . . . that every mouth may be stopped, and all the world may become guilty before God" (Rom. 3:19). My friend, you and I are lawbreakers, we are sinners needing a Savior. The thing to do is to receive Christ as your *Savior* before He comes as the Sovereign of this universe when He will be your *Judge*.

Now, going back to the verse we have been considering, "this gospel of the kingdom shall be preached in all the world for a witness unto all nations; and then shall the end come." This does not mean that while the church is here in the world the end can't come until the gospel of the grace of God is preached worldwide. I know there are those who use this verse to promote their Bible-teaching programs. While it is laudable to want to get the gospel to the ends of the earth, this is not the verse to use to promote it. You see, my friend, it is important to interpret Scripture in its context. Remember that our Lord is answering the question, "What is the sign of the end of the age?" (see v. 3). He is speaking of that end time.

THE GREAT TRIBULATION WITH ITS TROUBLE AND SORROWS

Now Jesus gives the sign that will identify this period of time.

When ye therefore shall see the abomination of desolation, spoken of by Daniel the prophet, stand in the holy place, (whoso readeth, let him understand:) [Matt. 24:15].

What is the abomination of desolation? Well, Daniel tells us about two of them. One of them was Antiochus Epiphanes, the Syrian, who came down and destroyed Jerusalem. In Daniel 11:31 we read: "And arms shall stand on his part, and they shall pollute the sanctuary of strength, and shall take away the daily sacrifice, and they shall place the abomination that maketh desolate." History bears out the fact that Antiochus Epiphanes came against Jerusalem in 170 B.C., at which time over one hundred thousand Jews were slain. He took away the daily sacrifice from the temple, offered the blood and broth of a swine upon the altar, and set up an image of Jupiter to be worshiped in the holy place.

However, our Lord is undoubtedly referring to the second abomination of desolation to which Daniel alludes (see Dan. 12:11), and I believe that it will be an image of Antichrist which will be set up in the temple. During the Tribulation the temple will be rebuilt and the nation of Israel will be back in Palestine. Obviously, our Lord is speaking of the temple rather than the church, because the church has no holy place. However, we cannot be certain that this is the abomination of desolation to which our Lord refers in the passage before us; this is just our surmising.

I am not looking for the abomination of desolation—I wouldn't know it if I met it on the street—but the people in the last days will be looking for it because it will be the sign to prove that they are in the Great Tribulation period. Instead of our looking for Antichrist and his abominations, we are told to be "Looking for that blessed hope, and the glorious appearing of the great God and our Saviour Jesus Christ" (Titus 2:13).

Our Lord says, "(whoso readeth, let him understand:)," which means the people who are living at that time *will* understand. Since you and I won't be there, He hasn't given us many details.

Now we are given another *time* word. When the abomination of desolation appears, "Then"—

Then let them which be in Judaea flee into the mountains [Matt. 24:16].

You and I are not expecting to flee to the mountains of Judea. I live very near the San Gabriel Mountains, and my neighbor tells me that if an atom bomb is dropped in Southern California, he is going to head for a certain canyon up there (and I may follow him!), but that will not fulfill this prophecy. In fact, it has nothing whatever to do with it. Rather, it has to do with people who are in Judea. Our Lord is giving that prophecy to those people, not to us.

Let him which is on the housetop not come down to take any thing out of his house [Matt. 24:17].

The housetop in Palestine corresponds to our front porch or our patio. Again let me emphasize the fact that our Lord is speaking to the folk in Palestine, not to you and me. This warning is not applicable to us; we don't spend our time on our housetops!

Neither let him which is in the field return back to take his clothes [Matt. 24:18].

This refers to people engaged in agriculture. If a worker in the fields leaves his cloak at the end of the row in the early morning when it is cool, and the word comes that the abomination of desolation has appeared, he is not to go back and get his cloak, but he is to start running.

And woe unto them that are with child, and to them that give suck in those days! [Matt. 24:19].

This reveals His great care and concern for mothers and little children. It will be a time when one should not have children.

It is believed that there will be a great population explosion at the beginning of the Great Tribulation. The fact that this earth is becoming overweighted with people in our day may be another evidence that we are approaching the end of the age.

But pray ye that your flight be not in the winter, neither on the sabbath day [Matt. 24:20].

Again, these are people who are observing the Sabbath day, which is Saturday. This is another proof that Christ is speaking directly to the Jewish people. I don't go to church on the Sabbath but on Sunday because my Lord rose from the dead on that day.

For then shall be great tribulation, such as was not since the beginning of the world to this time, no, nor ever shall be [Matt. 24:21].

"For then shall be great tribulation"—in Revelation 7:14 the literal translation is "the tribulation the great one," placing the article before both the noun and the adjective for emphasis. In other words, this tribulation is unique; there has been nothing like it in the history of the world, and there will never again be anything like it. And notice that our Lord is the One who labels the end of the age as the Great Tribulation. (If you want to find fault with it, talk to Him, not to me.)

"Such as was not since the beginning of the world to this time, no, nor ever shall be." Since that is true, believe me, people will know it when it gets here! I hear people today talking about the church going through the Tribulation, and they don't seem to realize how severe it will be. In fact, some folk say that we are in the Great Tribulation at the present time! Well, things are bad in our day, I'll grant that, but this period can be matched with many other periods in history. When the Great Tribulation gets here, there will be nothing to match it in the past or in the future.

And except those days should be shortened, there should no flesh be saved: but for the elect's sake those days shall be shortened [Matt. 24:22].

We read in the Book of Revelation that during the Tribulation one third of the population of the earth will be destroyed. On another occasion one-fourth of the population will be destroyed. It is absolutely unique. Using the simile given to us in Revelation 6, the red horse of war, the black horse of famine, and then the pale horse of death will ride during that period, and the population of the earth will be decimated. There was a time when this seemed to be an exaggeration. Even some good commentators considered it hyperbole. However, now that several nations of the world have atom bombs, which could destroy the population of the world, it no longer appears to be exaggerated.

However, there is comfort in this verse—"but for the elect's sake those days shall be shortened." God will not let mankind commit suicide. That is the reason this will be such a brief period.

JESUS ASSURES THEM CONCERNING HIS COMING AGAIN

Now we come to what will be the sign of His coming.

> **Then if any man shall say unto you, Lo, here is Christ, or there; believe it not.**
>
> **For there shall arise false Christs, and false prophets, and shall shew great signs and wonders; insomuch that, if it were possible, they shall deceive the very elect.**
>
> **Behold, I have told you before [Matt. 24:23–25].**

Don't miss what He is saying here. The ability to work miracles in our day should be looked upon with suspicion because the next great miracle worker will not be Christ; he will be Antichrist with his false prophets.

"If it were possible they shall deceive the very elect." Who are the elect? In the Scriptures there are two elect groups: the elect of the nation Israel and the elect of the church. We have to use common sense to determine which group is meant. Who has our Lord been talking about up to this point? Israel. All right, Israel is the elect in this verse, also. Jesus is not talking about the church. You can fool some of the people some of the time. You can fool all of the people some of the time. But you cannot fool God's children all of the time. It just can't be done. I have read many letters which testify of this. A recent letter is from a woman who has come out of a religious cult. She listened to our Bible-teaching radio program for months before she could see the error of the cult's teaching. It isn't possible to fool God's children all the time. They will come out of a cult eventually.

> **Wherefore if they shall say unto you, Behold, he is in the desert; go not forth: behold, he is in the secret chambers; believe it not.**
>
> **For as the lightning cometh out of the east, and shineth even unto the west; so shall also the coming of the Son of man be [Matt. 24:26–27].**

When He comes, there will not be any John the Baptist to announce Him. But when He comes, the whole world will know and it will be as public as lightning. Those of you that live in the Middle West know that a lightning storm is a public affair. When it comes, everybody knows about it, and sometimes it is a frightful experience. The Lord's second coming to the earth will be like that. No one will need to announce it. When our Lord comes the second time to establish His Kingdom on earth, everyone will know He is coming. (Remember that His second coming to earth does not refer to the Rapture.)

> **For wheresoever the carcase is, there will the eagles be gathered together [Matt. 24:28].**

This is the most difficult verse to understand in the entire Olivet Discourse. After speaking of His coming in glory like lightning out of heaven, then to speak of carrion-eating birds seems strange indeed. But I believe it refers to Christ's coming in judgment, because Revelation 19 tells us about an invitation that went out to the birds to come together for a great banquet, "And I saw an angel standing in the sun; and he cried with a loud voice, saying to all the fowls that fly in the midst of heaven, Come and gather yourselves together unto the supper of the great God; That ye may eat the flesh of kings, and the flesh of captains, and the flesh of mighty men, and the flesh of horses, and of them that sit on them, and the flesh of all men, both free and bond, both small and great. And I saw the beast, and the kings of the earth, and their armies, gathered together to make war against him that sat on the horse, and against his army" (Rev. 19:17–19). The birds that feed on carrion seem to be agents of divine judgment. When the Lord comes again, He will come in judgment.

> **Immediately after the tribulation of those days shall the
> sun be darkened, and the moon shall not give her light,
> and the stars shall fall from heaven, and the powers of
> the heavens shall be shaken [Matt. 24:29].**

Notice that this is to be "Immediately *after* the tribulation of those
days." It is my understanding that all of these things will take place at
Christ's second coming to the earth.

> **And then shall appear the sign of the Son of man in
> heaven: and then shall all the tribes of the earth mourn,
> and they shall see the Son of man coming in the clouds
> of heaven with power and great glory [Matt. 24:30].**

"Then shall appear the sign of the Son of man in heaven." What is that
sign? Again I will have to speculate. Back in the Old Testament, you
remember, the nation Israel was given the glory, the *Shekinah* presence of God. No other nation or people has ever had that, nor does the
church have it. The *Shekinah* glory rested over the tabernacle and
later the temple at Jerusalem. But because of Israel's sin, the *Shekinah*
glory left the nation. When Christ came the first time, He laid aside,
not His deity, but His prerogative of deity, His glory—although John
says, " . . . we beheld his glory . . ." (John 1:14), because there were
times when it broke through. However, at His second coming, I believe that the *Shekinah* glory will hover over the earth before He
breaks through, and that will be the "sign of the Son of man in
heaven."

"They shall see the Son of man coming in the clouds of heaven
with power and great glory." This is His return to earth to set up His
kingdom.

> **And he shall send his angels with a great sound of a
> trumpet, and they shall gather together his elect from
> the four winds, from one end of heaven to the other
> [Matt. 24:31].**

The elect spoken of in this verse is still the nation Israel. The prophets in the Old Testament foretold of a miracle that would bring the Jews back into their land. (This is not the church which is going to be caught up out of this world to meet the Lord in the air. Angels are not connected with the Rapture.) The Lord will come in person to receive the church with the sound of a trumpet, and His voice will be like that of an archangel. He will not need any help to gather His church together. He died for the church, and He will bring it together. When He says that the "angels . . . shall gather together his elect from the four winds, from one end of heaven to the other," we can be sure that He is talking about the nation Israel—ministering angels have always been connected with Israel.

THE PARABLE OF THE FIG TREE AS A SIGN

Now learn a parable of the fig tree; When his branch is yet tender, and putteth forth leaves, ye know that summer is nigh:

So likewise ye, when ye shall see all these things, know that it is near, even at the doors [Matt. 24:32–33].

I don't see how the fig tree could represent anything other than the nation Israel (e.g., see Jer. 24; Hos. 9:10). There are certainly fig trees growing in abundance in Israel even in our day after all that has happened to that land. I was impressed with the fig orchards north of Jerusalem and the vineyards south of Jerusalem—the area south of Bethlehem is filled with vineyards. Fig trees and grapevines identify the land, and I believe that our Lord is using the fig tree as a symbol of that land.

Verily I say unto you, This generation shall not pass, till all these things be fulfilled [Matt. 24:34].

"This generation"—the Greek word can mean race and refer to the nation Israel. Or it could refer to the generation that will be living at the time these predictions come to pass. A generation is reckoned to be about twenty years, and certainly the predicted events of this section will take place in a much briefer time than twenty years. My feeling is that it could refer to either one, but I much prefer the interpretation that it refers to the preservation of the Jewish race. Haman was not able to destroy them, neither was Pharaoh, nor did Hitler succeed in his attempts. And no dictator in our day will be able to exterminate these people—God will see to that.

> **Heaven and earth shall pass away, but my words shall not pass away [Matt. 24:35].**

He says, "You can just underscore what I've said, because heaven and earth will pass away, but My words will not." Heaven and earth will pass away; there will be a new heaven and a new earth (see Rev. 21:1), but He will not change His Word; it will stand throughout the eternal ages.

> **But of that day and hour knoweth no man, no, not the angels of heaven, but my Father only [Matt. 24:36].**

Although they will know that this period is drawing near, they will not know the day nor the hour. Since there have been so many folk in our day who have tried to pinpoint the time of Christ's return, I'm of the opinion that in that future day there will be some folk who will try to figure it down to the very hour. But no one will know either the day or the hour. And He will use the illustration of Noah—

> **But as the days of Noe were, so shall also the coming of the Son of man be [Matt. 24:37].**

Christ will come in a day which will be like the days of Noah.

> **For as in the days that were before the flood they were eating and drinking, marrying and giving in marriage, until the day that Noe entered into the ark,**

And knew not until the flood came, and took them all away; so shall also the coming of the Son of man be [Matt. 24:38–39].

Now, the days of Noah were characterized by gross immorality—every thought and imagination of man's heart was only evil continually (see Gen. 6:5). But our Lord says that His coming will be in days like the days of Noah, and He mentions only that they were eating and drinking. Is there anything wrong with eating and drinking? No, we are told that whatever we do—whether we eat or drink, or whatsoever we do, we are to do all to the glory of God (see 1 Cor. 10:31). However, the people in Noah's day were not eating and drinking to the glory of God. In fact, they were living as though God did not exist.

A little boy was invited out to dinner for the first time in his life. He was just going next door, but to him it was a big event. So when the time came to go, he made a beeline for the house next door. When they sat down to the table to eat, the boy automatically bowed his head to offer thanks for the food because he came from a Christian home. Suddenly he realized he was the only one with a bowed head and the rest of the folk were passing food back and forth. He opened his eyes and, not having any inhibitions, said, "Don't you thank God for your food?" There was embarrassing silence for a moment, and then the lady of the house said, "No, we don't." The little fellow thought for a moment and then said, "You're like my dogs—they just start right in!"

In our day there are multitudes of people who receive a meal that comes from the hand of God three times a day while millions of people are starving to death, and they never think of thanking God. And in that future day, they will be right on the verge of the coming of Christ, and they will be living as though it will never take place.

Also, the people of Noah's day were "marrying and giving in marriage." Certainly our Lord is not saying that marriage is wrong. His point is that they rejected so completely God's warning through Noah that they went ahead and had their weddings—maybe even "church" weddings—right up to the day that Noah entered into the ark. They lived as though God did not exist. They did not believe that He would judge them and scorned the warning that a flood was imminent. "And

knew not until the flood came, and took them all away; so shall also
the coming of the Son of man be."

> **Then shall two be in the field; the one shall be taken,
> and the other left.**

> **Two women shall be grinding at the mill; the one shall
> be taken, and the other left [Matt. 24:40–41].**

I can hear someone saying to me, "Well, preacher, you have finally
painted yourself into a corner. You said the church and the Rapture are
not in the Olivet Discourse, but here they are. Two shall be in the
field; one shall be taken, and the other shall be left."

Well, my friend, He still is not talking about the Rapture. After all,
what is our Lord talking about here? "As the days of Noe were." Who
was taken away in the days of Noah? "They knew not until the flood
came, and took them *all* away." They perished in the Flood. This is not
referring to the Rapture when the church will be taken out of the
world. Rather, this pictures the removing from the earth by judgment
those who are not going to enter the millennial Kingdom.

> **Watch therefore: for ye know not what hour your Lord
> doth come [Matt. 24:42].**

Watch is the important word, and it has a little different meaning from
the watching that the child of God does now in waiting for the Rapture. Today we have a comforting hope. In that future day it will be
watching with fear and anxiety. In the night they will say, "Would to
God it were morning," and in the morning they will say, "Would to
God it were evening." Today we are to wait and long for His coming. In
that future day they will watch with anxiety for His return.

You may think that I am splitting hairs, but I'm not. I looked up the
Greek word for *watch* and found that it had about eight different
meanings. Although in English we have only the one word, it has
several different meanings, also.

Let me illustrate this by a man who goes deer hunting. Every year this man goes into the woods to about the same spot. He puts up camp, and early in the morning he goes over the hogback on the hill and sits down by the trunk of an old tree and waits. After a while he hears a noise in the brush and thinks it might be a deer. He lifts his rifle and waits. He is watching for a deer.

Two weeks later you meet this same man down on the main street corner of town, and you see that he is looking intently down the street. You know that he is waiting for someone. You walk up to him and say, "Who are you watching for?" He replies, "I'm waiting for my wife; she is forty-five minutes late." He is watching for a dear again, but it is a different deer and he is watching in a little different way. Before, on the hill, he had his deer gun with him, and he sort of wishes he had it with him again, but it is against the law for him to shoot her! But he is watching, and watching in a different way, you see.

A month or two later you go to the hospital and you pass a room and see this man and his wife sitting by the bedside of a little child. The child has a burning fever, and the doctor has told them that the crisis will come about midnight. They are watching. My friend, that is a different type of watching than watching for a deer or waiting for a wife on the corner. This is watching with anxiety. And I think it will be somewhat with the same feeling that they will watch for our Lord's second coming.

> **But know this, that if the goodman of the house had known in what watch the thief would come, he would have watched, and would not have suffered his house to be broken up.**

> **Therefore be ye also ready: for in such an hour as ye think not the Son of man cometh.**

> **Who then is a faithful and wise servant, whom his lord hath made ruler over his household, to give them meat in due season? [Matt. 24:43–45].**

What our Lord is doing in the remainder of the Olivet Discourse is giving parables to illustrate the attitude of folk to His coming and what will happen when He does come.

> **Blessed is that servant, whom his lord when he cometh shall find so doing.**
>
> **Verily I say unto you, That he shall make him ruler over all his goods.**
>
> **But and if that evil servant shall say in his heart, My lord delayeth his coming;**
>
> **And shall begin to smite his fellowservants, and to eat and drink with the drunken;**
>
> **The lord of that servant shall come in a day when he looketh not for him, and in an hour that he is not aware of,**
>
> **And shall cut him asunder, and appoint him his portion with the hypocrites: there shall be weeping and gnashing of teeth [Matt. 24:46–51].**

This parable reflects the attitude of some folk in that future day. They shall say, "Well, the Lord delays His coming—so I'll just go on living carelessly." When Christ returns, He will judge that man.

This is a great principle which is applicable to every age. You and I ought to live our lives in the light of the fact that we are to stand in the presence of Christ. Note that I didn't say in the light of the *coming* of Christ but in the light of the *presence* of Christ. Regardless of whether Christ comes a hundred years from today or a thousand years, you and I will stand in His presence. Whether you are saved or lost, you will stand in His presence. If you are saved, you will have to give Him an account of your life to see if you receive a reward. If you are lost, you will stand there to be judged. Therefore, every person should live his life in light of the fact that he is to stand in the presence of the Lord.

This is the great emphasis in the Olivet Discourse. Therefore, it has applications to us, although the interpretation is specifically to folk living at the time of Christ's return as King.

CHART OF OLIVET DISCOURSE

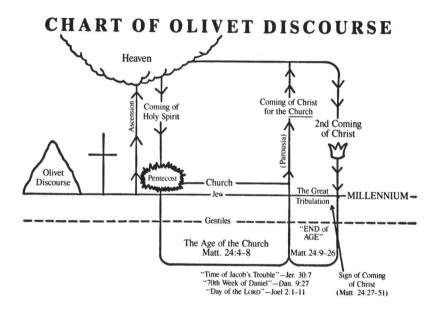

Heaven

Coming of Christ for the Church

Ascension

Coming of Holy Spirit

2nd Coming of Christ

(Parousia)

Olivet Discourse

Pentecost

Church

Jew

The Great Tribulation

MILLENNIUM

Gentiles

"END of AGE"

The Age of the Church
Matt. 24:4–8

Matt. 24:9–26

"Time of Jacob's Trouble"—Jer. 30:7
"70th Week of Daniel"—Dan. 9:27
"Day of the LORD"—Joel 2:1-11

Sign of Coming of Christ
(Matt. 24:27-51)

CHAPTER 25

THEME: *Olivet Discourse continued—the parable of the ten virgins, the talents, and the judgment of the gentile nations*

This chapter enlarges upon the answer of Jesus to the question, "What shall be the sign of thy coming?" (Matt. 24:3). There is the parable of the ten virgins, which tests the genuineness of the faith of Israel; the parable of the talents, which tests the faithfulness of His servants; and the judgment of the gentile nations, which tests their right of admission into the Kingdom. This chapter shows the significance of the coming of Christ as it relates to these groups that shall then be in the world. A close analysis of each group will reveal that it can be stripped down to a personal attitude and relationship to Jesus Christ.

The parable of the ten virgins is the basis for those who believe in what is known as the partial rapture, where only some will be taken out of the world. The "partial rapture" group is made up of very fine people. When I first became pastor in Nashville, Tennessee, there was a wonderful Bible class there, and they supported me in getting Bible conferences into Nashville. From the beginning, the class had been taught by a teacher who believed in a partial rapture. Candidly, I feel that the partial rapture theory ministers to spiritual snobbery. I never met one of that group who didn't think that he was with the five wise virgins. In fact, I have never in all my life met one who thought he was classed with the foolish virgins! I was a young preacher in those days, and as I worked with them I had the feeling that they were not sure that I was one of them. I suspected that they classified me as one of the foolish ones.

I thank God that when the Rapture takes place, every believer is going out. And we won't be going on the basis of merit. All of us will be leaving because of the grace of God. He saves us by grace; He keeps us by grace; He will take us out of this world by grace; and when we have been there for ten million years, it will be by the grace of God.

The ten virgins do not refer to the church, they refer to the nation Israel. My friend, we need to let our Lord answer the questions of these men who were His apostles. They had asked Him the questions. If we try to make out that He is talking to us about something altogether different, it is as though we are interrupting Him. Let's just listen and know that, although He is talking to someone else, we can make application of these wonderful parables to our own lives.

PARABLE OF THE TEN VIRGINS

Then shall the kingdom of heaven be likened unto ten virgins, which took their lamps, and went forth to meet the bridegroom [Matt. 25:1].

To better understand the customs in Israel during the New Testament period, we refer to the Peshitta, which is a Syriac version of the Bible. Although it is not a text to be recommended, it does shed light on some of the customs of the day. The Peshitta translation of the verse before us indicates that the virgins went forth to meet the bridegroom *and the bride*, which means that the bridegroom is coming from the marriage to the marriage supper. It is my understanding that, although the marriage of Christ and the church takes place in heaven, the marriage supper takes place on this earth. A passage in the Gospel of Luke substantiates this. As our Lord is giving warnings and parables, He says, "Let your loins be girded about, and your lights burning; And ye yourselves like unto men that wait for their lord, when he will return from the wedding; that when he cometh and knocketh, they may open unto him immediately" (Luke 12:35–36). You see, the wedding has taken place, and the bride is with him. Obviously, if he is coming from the wedding, the bride is with him; no man ever went on a honeymoon by himself—if he did, it wasn't a honeymoon!

So here in the parable of the ten virgins, Christ, pictured as the bridegroom, is bringing the bride with Him, and the believers on earth are waiting for Him to come. While the Great Tribulation has been going on upon the earth, Christ has been yonder in heaven with

His bride, the church. Then at the conclusion of the seven years of Tribulation, He comes back to earth with the church.

This, now, is the attitude toward His coming on the part of those on the earth—

> **And five of them were wise, and five were foolish.**
>
> **They that were foolish took their lamps, and took no oil with them:**
>
> **But the wise took oil in their vessels with their lamps [Matt. 25:2–4].**

Oil is symbolic of the Spirit of God. In that day I think there will be phonies as there were at His first coming. Jesus called them hypocrites. They will have lamps but no oil.

> **While the bridegroom tarried, they all slumbered and slept.**
>
> **And at midnight there was a cry made, Behold, the bridegroom cometh; go ye out to meet him.**
>
> **Then all those virgins arose, and trimmed their lamps [Matt. 25:5–7].**

Notice that *both* the wise and the foolish virgins slept. The difference in them was that some had the Holy Spirit (represented by the oil) and some did not—because they were not genuine believers.

Our Lord concludes this parable with a warning—

> **Watch therefore, for ye know neither the day nor the hour wherein the Son of man cometh [Matt. 25:13].**

Notice that it is "the day nor the hour" rather than the century or the year, as it is from our perspective. The attitude for His own during this future period is to *watch*. That is the important thing for them to do.

PARABLE OF THE TALENTS

This is another parable for that future generation that will be waiting for our Lord's return to earth.

> **For the kingdom of heaven is as a man travelling into a far country, who called his own servants, and delivered unto them his goods.**

> **And unto one he gave five talents, to another two, and to another one; to every man according to his several ability; and straightway took his journey [Matt. 25:14–15].**

Notice that the master gave to his servants responsibilities according to their individual abilities.

> **Then he that had received the five talents went and traded with the same, and made them other five talents.**

> **And likewise he that had received two, he also gained other two [Matt. 25:16–17].**

Notice that the "talents" were sums of money. They do not represent talents in the sense of the natural endowments of a person such as a musical talent. The application to us is that whatever God has given to us, we are to use for Him.

> **But he that had received one went and digged in the earth, and hid his lord's money [Matt. 25:18].**

All were given a certain sum of money and told to use it profitably. But one buried the talent he had been given. He was not faithful to his master.

> **After a long time the lord of those servants cometh, and reckoneth with them.**

And so he that had received five talents came and brought other five talents, saying, Lord, thou deliveredst unto me five talents: behold, I have gained beside them five talents more.

His lord said unto him, Well done, thou good and faithful servant: thou hast been faithful over a few things, I will make thee ruler over many things: enter thou into the joy of thy lord.

He also that had received two talents came and said, Lord, thou deliveredst unto me two talents: behold, I have gained two other talents beside them.

His lord said unto him, Well done, good and faithful servant; thou hast been faithful over a few things, I will make thee ruler over many things: enter thou into the joy of thy lord.

Then he which had received the one talent came and said, Lord, I knew thee that thou art an hard man, reaping where thou hast not sown, and gathering where thou hast not strawed:

And I was afraid, and went and hid thy talent in the earth: lo, there thou hast that is thine [Matt. 25:19–25].

The response of his master was this—

His lord answered and said unto him, Thou wicked and slothful servant, thou knewest that I reap where I sowed not, and gather where I have not strawed:

Thou oughtest therefore to have put my money to the exchangers, and then at my coming I should have received mine own with usury.

Take therefore the talent from him, and give it unto him which hath ten talents.

> **For unto every one that hath shall be given, and he shall have abundance: but from him that hath not shall be taken away even that which he hath.**
>
> **And cast ye the unprofitable servant into outer darkness: there shall be weeping and gnashing of teeth [Matt. 25:26–30].**

There is a great principle in this parable for us. And it was given in the light of the fact that all of us—you and I included—are going to have to stand in the presence of God and give an account of how we have used what He has given to us. The Lord is not going to ask us how *much* we have done for Him but how *faithful* we have been to that which He wanted us to do.

For the child of God there are two important things: (1) Find out what God wants us to do; that is, determine what the talent is that He has given us, and then (2) be faithful in the use of it. To some of us God gives a very small ministry, and that may be upsetting to us; but if we are one-talent people, God expects us to be *faithful* with that.

JUDGMENT OF THE NATIONS

In this chapter our Lord is alerting God's people to the fact that we are to ready ourselves for His coming. This is certainly true in the next few verses.

During the Tribulation period all nations will have the opportunity to hear and receive God's message. The gospel of the Kingdom will be preached among all nations, we are told. But some will reject God's messengers, Christ's brethren, and thereby reject Christ.

> **When the Son of man shall come in his glory, and all the holy angels with him, then shall he sit upon the throne of his glory [Matt. 25:31].**

The polarization of all of the Olivet Discourse is moving toward the placing of Jesus Christ on the throne of this world. This is the message of the Gospel of Matthew—in fact, it is the message of the entire Word of God.

Now we will see that the nations will be judged. You may ask, "Doesn't it mean individuals?" Yes, you can consider it as individuals composing the nations. But nations are responsible to God.

And before him shall be gathered all nations: and he shall separate them one from another, as a shepherd divideth his sheep from the goats [Matt. 25:32].

"Nation"is the Greek word *ethnos,* we could say that it means ethnic groups.

And he shall set the sheep on his right hand, but the goats on the left [Matt. 25:33].

I do not know of an instance when God calls individuals *goats.* All human beings are called sheep. There are two kinds: lost sheep and saved sheep. "All we like sheep have gone astray; we have turned every one to his own way; and the LORD hath laid on him the iniquity of us all" (Isa. 53:6). There are lost sheep and saved sheep, not sheep and goats. I believe that the goats represent groups of nations.

Now notice what the test is—

Then shall the King say unto them on his right hand, Come, ye blessed of my Father, inherit the kingdom prepared for you from the foundation of the world:

For I was an hungered, and ye gave me meat: I was thirsty, and ye gave me drink: I was a stranger, and ye took me in:

Naked, and ye clothed me: I was sick, and ye visited me: I was in prison, and ye came unto me.

> Then shall the righteous answer him, saying, Lord, when saw we thee an hungered, and fed thee? or thirsty, and gave thee drink?
>
> When saw we thee a stranger, and took thee in? or naked, and clothed thee?
>
> Or when saw we thee sick, or in prison, and came unto thee?
>
> And the King shall answer and say unto them, Verily I say unto you, Inasmuch as ye have done it unto one of the least of these my brethren, ye have done it unto me [Matt. 25:34–40].

The 144,000 Jews sealed at the time of the Great Tribulation will go out over the entire world to preach the message of the gospel of the Kingdom, which is to receive Christ as the sacrifice for their sins and to be ready for His immediate coming. Some nations will reject Christ. Antichrist will have God's messengers butchered and slain, and anyone who would give them a cup of cold water will do so at the risk of his life. To hand out a cup of cold water has little value in our day, but in the Great Tribulation it will have tremendous value. It will mean taking a stand for Jesus Christ. The basis on which the nations will be judged is their acceptance or rejection of Jesus Christ. He says, "Inasmuch as ye have done it unto one of the least of these my brethren, ye have done it unto me"—because the messengers were representing Him. That will be the way they evidence faith in the message that the Kingdom of Heaven is at hand and that they are to repent and turn to Christ to be saved.

For those who reject, there is only judgment—

> Then shall he answer them, saying, Verily I say unto you, Inasmuch as ye did it not to one of the least of these, ye did it not to me.

And these shall go away into everlasting punishment:
but the righteous into life eternal [Matt. 25:45–46].

Entire nations will enter the millennial Kingdom. Out of these will be some individuals who will reject Christ. But the judgment of the nations at the second coming of Christ is to determine what nations are to enter the millennial Kingdom. This judgment is separate and distinct from all other judgments.

CHAPTER 26

THEME: Final events in the life of Jesus immediately before the Cross; the plot to arrest Him; the anointing by Mary of Bethany; the selling by Judas Iscariot; the celebration of the first Lord's Supper; the predicted denial by Peter; the agony in the Garden of Gethsemane; the betrayal by Judas; the arrest by the chief priests; the trial before Caiaphas and the Sanhedrin; the denial by Peter

This is the longest chapter in the Gospel of Matthew. There is a break at the conclusion of verse 30. The events recorded in John 15—17 could be inserted here. Another natural break would be at the beginning of verse 57. A chapter division here would set the trial before the religious rulers in a separate category. Perhaps those who divided the Scriptures included so many events in one chapter to give the reader something of the scope and rapidity of these significant happenings.

Every incident and detail in this chapter points to the Cross. There is a trip-hammer precision here that may give the reader the impression that Jesus is caught in the vortex of circumstances over which He has no control. A careful examination and consideration, however, will reveal that He is the master of circumstances, and He is never more kingly than when He draws near the Cross.

All things recorded in this chapter and chapter 27 should be studied in the light of His determination at Caesarea Philippi—six months previously—to go to Jerusalem to die: "From that time forth began Jesus to shew unto his disciples, how that he must go unto Jerusalem, and suffer many things of the elders and chief priests and scribes, and be killed, and be raised again the third day" (Matt. 16:21).

He is moving according to God's timetable, and He is forcing the issue. He is not the helpless victim caught between the upper millstone of religious intrigue and the nether millstone of Roman power.

A reverence should pervade our thinking as we consider these things written in this chapter, for they are vitally related to our salvation.

PLAN TO KILL JESUS

And it came to pass, when Jesus had finished all these sayings, he said unto his disciples [Matt. 26:1].

"When Jesus had finished all these sayings"—what sayings? The Olivet Discourse. He has answered their questions regarding the end of the age, and now He has something else for them—

Ye know that after two days is the feast of the passover, and the Son of man is betrayed to be crucified [Matt. 26:2].

Now let's read ahead to verse 5 and see something very interesting here—

Then assembled together the chief priests, and the scribes, and the elders of the people, unto the palace of the high priest, who was called Caiaphas,

And consulted that they might take Jesus by subtilty, and kill him.

But they said, Not on the feast day, lest there be an uproar among the people [Matt 26:3–5].

In verse 2 Jesus tells His disciples that He is going to die. According to the record, this is the sixth time He has told them. Six months before this, beginning at Caesarea Philippi, He announced His impending death. And now He sets the *time* of His death. He tells them that He will die during the Passover. But the religious rulers had other plans—notice verse 5. "But *they* said, Not on the feast day lest there be an uproar among the people." The very ones who put Him to death said that they would *not* crucify Him during the Passover; *He* said that He would die during the Passover. When did He die? He died during the Passover. You see, Jesus, not His enemies, set the time of His execution. He is in command; He is the King in Matthew's Gospel, and when He seems more helpless and weak than at any other time, He still is in charge. The bitter hatred of His enemies had led them to plot His murder, and they wanted to do it their way, but they will not be permitted to do that. The closer Jesus gets to the Cross, the more kingly He becomes.

We pass from that incident to one of marvelous light.

JESUS IS ANOINTED BY MARY OF BETHANY

Now when Jesus was in Bethany, in the house of Simon the leper,

There came unto him a woman having an alabaster box of very precious ointment, and poured it on his head, as he sat at meat [Matt. 26:6–7].

Bethany was the place of love, as Jerusalem was the place of hate. He stayed in Bethany during His last hours before His death. This incident took place in the home of Simon the leper. Why did they call him Simon the leper? Did he have leprosy? There was a time when he had this disease, but Jesus had undoubtedly healed him. Now he is able to sit down and have fellowship with the Lord Jesus and others who are having dinner with him at his home. This is a wonderful scene, my friend. The Lord's enemies today do not know Him. They do not know the Lord who healed, who loved, who wept and judged. In fact, some of His enemies of today recently presented a play in a local college in which Jesus and His disciples were characterized as sinful men! Our laws have banned prayer and Bible reading in schools, but they permit the dirtiest, filthiest portrayals of our Lord, and outright blasphemy! Of course, those who produce such things are ignorant; they don't know our Lord. In fact, they are spiritual lepers. If they told the truth, they would have to say of themselves, "Unclean, unclean!"

When you have come to the Lord Jesus and have been cleansed by

Him, you can sit down and have fellowship with Him. This is the scene we have in this passage. As they were having dinner, a woman (John 12:3 tells us that it was Mary) came to Jesus with an alabaster box of precious ointment and anointed both His head and His feet with fragrant ointment. John also tells us that it was Judas Iscariot who led the agitation against her, although all the disciples agreed with him.

> **But when his disciples saw it, they had indignation, saying, To what purpose is this waste? [Matt. 26:8].**

I wonder how much they really cared about the poor. They remind me of folk in our contemporary society who are always talking about taking care of the poor but are doing nothing about it themselves. In our government there are quite a few legislators who are millionaires and are always talking about a poverty program and other aid for the poor. Have you ever attempted to find out how much they personally have done for the poor? I don't care for that kind of hypocrisy! The evidence of the sincerity of your concern is always in what you yourself are doing. Are you trying to make an impression, or are you really trying to help folk?

> **For this ointment might have been sold for much, and given to the poor [Matt. 26:9].**

That is accurate—it could have been. It is estimated that the cost of it equalled a year's salary for a rural worker.

> **When Jesus understood it, he said unto them, Why trouble ye the woman? for she hath wrought a good work upon me [Matt. 26:10].**

As far as Christians are concerned, they should not give to anything nor do anything that does not glorify the name of the Lord Jesus Christ. Personally, I refuse to participate in any so-called good works in the community unless Christ is glorified in them, unless they are done in His name. And I am amazed at how little they really accomplish. How much do they really give that brings blessing to people? It makes me sick when I hear of the corruption among the politicians in the poverty programs. However, when loving assistance is given in the name of the Lord Jesus, He Himself said that it was a good work.

For ye have the poor always with you; but me ye have not always [Matt. 26:11].

Those of us who say we trust Christ and want to honor and glorify Him ought to be doing *more* in His name today.

For in that she hath poured this ointment on my body, she did it for my burial.

Verily I say unto you, Wheresoever this gospel shall be preached in the whole world, there shall also this, that this woman hath done, be told for a memorial of her [Matt. 26:12–13].

That home of Simon the leper in Bethany was a place of light and friendship for the Lord Jesus. In contrast, Jerusalem was the place of hatred. He did not spend a night in the city of Jerusalem during that final week, but He went out to Bethany and stayed with these folk who loved Him. Those who want Him, who love Him, are the ones He fellowships with in our day. My friend, you can have Him if you want Him.

The beautiful story of the broken alabaster box has filled the world with its fragrance. Our Lord said, "Wheresoever this gospel shall be preached in the whole world, there shall also this, that this woman hath done, be told for a memorial of her." And we are telling it right now. I hear folk speak about being in the apostolic succession, but I would like to be in the succession of Mary. Mary alone, of all Christ's followers, understood and entered into His death, while the apostles missed the point completely. Although she stood on the fringe of things, she understood, and to let Him know, she anointed Him. Did she waste her ointment? In the Gospel records I read that on the morning of that first day of the week other women came to the tomb of Jesus to anoint His body for burial. I have a question to ask you: Did they put their ointment on the body of Jesus? No, He wasn't in that tomb—He was risen. Mary alone had the privilege of anointing Him. My friend, you and I need to break our alabaster box of ointment in the name of the Lord Jesus. The world outside doesn't know Him; so we ought to be very careful that what we do brings glory, not to ourselves, but to Him.

Now we turn from that beautiful scene of light to another dark scene.

PLOT OF JUDAS TO SELL JESUS

Then one of the twelve, called Judas Iscariot, went unto the chief priests,

And said unto them, What will ye give me, and I will deliver him unto you? And they covenanted with him for thirty pieces of silver.

And from that time he sought opportunity to betray him [Matt. 26:14–16].

This deed of Judas Iscariot is dark and dastardly in contrast to Mary's act of spiritual perception. Dante gave Judas and Brutus the lowest place in *The Inferno*, and no one since then has said he was wrong. These men did the lowest and basest thing men could do when they betrayed one to whom they should have been loyal.

"He sought opportunity to betray him." You see, the arrest had to take place when Jesus was alone—that is, when the crowds were gone. Judas waited for such a time.

THE PASSOVER AND THE LAST SUPPER

Now the first day of the feast of unleavened bread the disciples came to Jesus, saying unto him, Where wilt thou that we prepare for thee to eat the passover?

And he said, Go into the city to such a man, and say
unto him, The Master saith, My time is at hand; I will
keep the passover at thy house with my disciples.

And the disciples did as Jesus had appointed them; and
they made ready the passover [Matt. 26:17–19].

Now the Lord Jesus will go with His own into the Upper Room, and
there He will make the announcement that one will betray Him.

Now when the even was come, he sat down with the
twelve.

And as they did eat, he said, Verily I say unto you, that
one of you shall betray me.

And they were exceeding sorrowful, and began every
one of them to say unto him, Lord, is it I? [Matt.
26:20–22].

Everyone of those men knew that he had it within his heart to betray
Christ. Have you discovered that in your own heart and life? My
friend, you and I are just that low. You may say, "Oh, I wouldn't do
that!" Are you sure? I would betray Him within the next five minutes
if He didn't keep His hand on me—and you would, too. That ought to
keep us close to Him.

And he answered and said, He that dippeth his hand
with me in the dish, the same shall betray me.

The Son of man goeth as it is written of him: but woe
unto that man by whom the Son of man is betrayed! it
had been good for that man if he had not been born.

Then Judas, which betrayed him, answered and said,
Master, is it I? He said unto him, Thou hast said [Matt.
26:23–25].

It is interesting to note that Judas did not call Him *Lord* as the other disciples did (see v. 22). At this juncture Judas left the room, according to John's record: "He then having received the sop went immediately out: and it was night" (John 13:30).

> **And as they were eating, Jesus took bread, and blessed it, and brake it, and gave it to the disciples, and said, Take, eat; this is my body.**
>
> **And he took the cup, and gave thanks, and gave it to them, saying, Drink ye all of it;**
>
> **For this is my blood of the new testament, which is shed for many for the remission of sins [Matt. 26:26–28].**

Here we see the Lord instituting the Lord's Supper over the dying ashes of a fading feast, the Passover. The cup circulated seven times during the Passover. It was evidently at the last time that Jesus instituted the Lord's Supper. During the feast they sang the Hallel Psalms—Psalms 111 to 118. When you read them for your own spiritual profit, keep in mind that our Lord sang them on that auspicious night. At that last supper, He reared a new monument to Himself. It was not made of marble or bronze but was made of the temporary elements of bread and wine. *Both speak of His death until He comes again.*

> **But I say unto you, I will not drink henceforth of this fruit of the vine, until that day when I drink it new with you in my Father's kingdom [Matt. 26:29].**

The Passover will be reinstituted in the Millennium. The Lord said that He would drink the fruit of the vine again in the Kingdom. This means that apparently the Passover during that time will look back to His death on the Cross. The Passover, which had looked forward for centuries to His coming, will also during the Millennium look back to His coming.

And when they had sung an hymn, they went out into the mount of Olives [Matt. 26:30].

PREDICTION OF PETER'S DENIAL

Then saith Jesus unto them, All ye shall be offended because of me this night: for it is written, I will smite the shepherd, and the sheep of the flock shall be scattered abroad [Matt. 26:31].

This is a quotation from Zechariah's prophecy (see Zech. 13:7).

But after I am risen again, I will go before you into Galilee.

Peter answered and said unto him, Though all men shall be offended because of thee, yet will I never be offended [Matt. 26:32–33].

Peter's answer suggested that he did not trust the other disciples either but that the Lord could sure depend upon him! Peter's problem was that he didn't know himself, and that is the problem many of us have today.

Jesus said unto him, Verily I say unto thee, That this night, before the cock crow, thou shalt deny me thrice.

Peter said unto him, Though I should die with thee, yet will I not deny thee. Likewise also said all the disciples [Matt. 26:34–35].

It was early in the evening that Peter said he would not deny our Lord. Yes, he was even ready to die with the Lord. That same night before the cock crowed Peter denied Him, not once, but three times.

GETHSEMANE

Then cometh Jesus with them unto a place called Geth-semane, and saith unto the disciples, Sit ye here, while I go and pray yonder.

And he took with him Peter and the two sons of Zebedee, and began to be sorrowful and very heavy.

Then saith he unto them, My soul is exceeding sorrow-ful, even unto death: tarry ye here, and watch with me.

And he went a little farther, and fell on his face, and prayed, saying, O my Father, if it be possible, let this cup pass from me: nevertheless not as I will, but as thou wilt [Matt. 26:36–39].

We need to pay attention to the prayer that our Lord is praying here. "This cup" evidently represents His cross and the contents are the sins of the whole world. More than the death itself and the terrible suffering of crucifixion is something else that we do not seem to real-ize. It is this: Jesus, holy, harmless, and separate from sinners, was made sin for us. There on the Cross the sin of humanity was put on Him—not in some forensic or academic manner, but in reality. We cannot even imagine the horror He felt when that sin was placed upon Him. It was a horrendous experience for this One who was holy. No-tice that He was not asking to escape the Cross, but He was praying that God's will be done. It is impossible for you and me to enter into the full significance of Gethsemane, but I think it was there that He won the victory of Calvary. Undoubtedly, He was tempted by Satan in Gethsemane as truly as He was in the wilderness. Notice verse 42: "He went away again the second time, and prayed, saying, O my Father, if this cup may not pass away from me, except I drink it, thy will be done." He was accepting it. To say that our Lord was trying to avoid going to the Cross is not exactly true. In His humanity He felt a repug-nance and the awful horror of having the sins of the world placed upon Himself, and He recoiled for a moment from it. But He committed Himself to the Father. He came to do the Father's will.

Now let's look at the disciples who were in the garden with Him—Peter, James, and John. After His first prayer, He came back to them and found them sleeping—

> **And he cometh unto the disciples, and findeth them asleep, and saith unto Peter, What, could ye not watch with me one hour?**
>
> **Watch and pray, that ye enter not into temptation: the spirit indeed is willing, but the flesh is weak [Matt. 26:40–41].**

"Watch"—stay awake, be alert—"and pray, that ye enter not into temptation." What was the temptation? Who was going to tempt them? Satan was there. Jesus wrestled with an unseen foe—that is obvious. He overcame the enemy there in Gethsemane. The victory of Calvary was won in Gethsemane.

> **He went away again the second time, and prayed, saying, O my Father, if this cup may not pass away from me, except I drink it, thy will be done [Matt. 26:42].**

He commits Himself to the Father's will.

> **And he came and found them asleep again: for their eyes were heavy.**
>
> **And he left them, and went away again, and prayed the third time, saying the same words.**
>
> **Then cometh he to his disciples, and saith unto them, Sleep on now, and take your rest: behold, the hour is at hand, and the Son of man is betrayed into the hands of sinners [Matt. 26:43–45].**

"Sleep on now and take your rest." Obviously, there is an interval of time between this and the next verse. He didn't tell them to go to sleep and in the next breath tell them to get up. There was time for their nap, and they needed this rest. Notice how our Lord pays attention to the needs of their bodies. After they had slept awhile, He said—

> **Rise, let us be going: behold, he is at hand that doth betray me.**
>
> **And while he yet spake, lo, Judas, one of the twelve, came, and with him a great multitude with swords and staves, from the chief priests and elders of the people [Matt. 26:46–47].**

The fact that Judas, and also the enemies of Jesus, had witnessed many miracles makes them realize that Jesus has supernatural power and that He might use it. So when they come to arrest Him, they bring a whole crowd of armed men. Possibly the whole guard came to arrest Him.

> **Now he that betrayed him gave them a sign, saying, Whomsoever I shall kiss, that same is he: hold him fast [Matt. 26:48].**

That hot kiss of betrayal is one of the worst things in recorded history.

> **And forthwith he came to Jesus, and said, Hail, master; and kissed him.**
>
> **And Jesus said unto him, Friend, wherefore art thou come? Then came they, and laid hands on Jesus, and took him [Matt. 26:49–50].**

A kiss can either be a sign of acceptance or rejection (see Ps. 2:12). In this instance Judas bestowed a kiss of betrayal upon the Lord Jesus, and it was one of the most despicable acts of man. Some theologians contend that Judas was predestined to betray Jesus and could do nothing else. If this were true, Judas was nothing more than a robot. I believe Judas made up his own mind to betray our Lord and had every opportunity to change his plans. You may say, "Yes, but it was prophesied that he would betray Jesus." I have to agree with you. It was prophesied, and our Lord marked him out as the man. However, after Judas had fulfilled the prophecy, after Jesus was betrayed, Judas could have repented. Jesus gave Judas one final opportunity to repent and accept Him. Even after he gave Jesus that hot kiss of betrayal, Jesus called him, "Friend." Later, when Judas went to the temple and threw down the silver given to him to betray the Lord, he could have changed his mind. As the priests were taking Jesus to Pilate, Judas could have fallen down before Him and said, "Forgive me, Lord, I did not know what I was doing." The Lord would have forgiven him.

And, behold, one of them which were with Jesus stretched out his hand, and drew his sword, and struck a servant of the high priest's, and smote off his ear [Matt. 26:51].

We know who that was; it was Simon Peter. I think that he was trying to prove something. Earlier Peter had boasted that he would die protecting Jesus, but Jesus told him that he would deny Him that very night. Well, Peter got a sword somewhere, and he intended to protect his Lord. But Peter was a fisherman, not a swordsman. He sliced off the man's ear; but he wasn't after ears, he was after his head. He intended to lop off the man's head, but he almost missed him!

Then said Jesus unto him, Put up again thy sword into his place: for all they that take the sword shall perish with the sword.

Thinkest thou that I cannot now pray to my Father, and he shall presently give me more than twelve legions of angels? [Matt. 26:52–53].

In other words, "I don't need your little sword, Peter. I haven't come to put up a battle against the religious rulers. I have come to die for the sins of the world."

> **But how then shall the scriptures be fulfilled, that thus it must be? [Matt. 26:54].**

You see, our Lord is fulfilling Scripture. Matthew makes this very clear.

> **In that same hour said Jesus to the multitudes, Are ye come out as against a thief with swords and staves for to take me? I sat daily with you teaching in the temple, and ye laid no hold on me [Matt. 26:55].**

Previously, His hour had not yet come. But now His hour *has* come—

> **But all this was done, that the scriptures of the prophets might be fulfilled. Then all the disciples forsook him, and fled [Matt. 26:56].**

Jesus had predicted this. All of the disciples leave Him now.

PALACE OF THE HIGH PRIEST

> **And they that had laid hold on Jesus led him away to Caiaphas the high priest, where the scribes and the elders were assembled [Matt. 26:57].**

We find out later that the father-in-law of Caiaphas was really the instigator of all this. But Jesus must be brought to Caiaphas, the high priest, for the first charge. Because the religious rulers are going to ask Rome for the death penalty, they must determine that night what charge against Jesus they can bring when they go to Pilate in the morning.

But Peter followed him afar off unto the high priest's palace, and went in, and sat with the servants, to see the end [Matt. 26:58].

Simon Peter followed afar off. It is dangerous for any of us to follow Jesus afar off. We are told in John 18:15–16 that with the aid of John, Peter gained entrance to the courtyard. He waited there to "see the end," and in just a short while he would deny the Lord.

Now the chief priests, and elders, and all the council, sought false witness against Jesus, to put him to death;

But found none: yea, though many false witnesses came, yet found they none. At the last came two false witnesses [Matt. 26:59–60].

You see, because the religious rulers had no charge against the Lord Jesus, they had to find *false* witnesses. And the trouble with getting false witnesses was in finding one that could stand up under investigation. Pilate might be a little inquisitive (which he was) and ask a few annoying questions. Finally, they found two witnesses—

And said, This fellow said, I am able to destroy the temple of God, and to build it in three days [Matt. 26:61].

According to John 2:19–22, even the disciples misunderstood Jesus when He made the statement: "Destroy this temple, and in three days I will raise it up." They didn't understand it until after Jesus' resurrection. Evidently the false witness was a man who had been present at the time Jesus made the statement, but notice that he doesn't quote Him accurately.

And the high priest arose, and said unto him, Answerest thou nothing? what is it which these witness against thee? [Matt. 26:62].

He tries to get the Lord Jesus to answer so the Sanhedrin will know what kind of an argument to use. The accusation is so absolutely far-fetched that our Lord does not answer it.

> **But Jesus held his peace. And the high priest answered and said unto him, I adjure thee by the living God, that thou tell us whether thou be the Christ, the Son of God [Matt. 26:63].**

Now the high priest puts Him on oath and asks Him the specific question, "Are you the Christ, the Son of God?"

> **Jesus saith unto him, Thou hast said: nevertheless I say unto you, Hereafter shall ye see the Son of man sitting on the right hand of power, and coming in the clouds of heaven [Matt. 26:64].**

"Jesus saith unto him, Thou hast said"—this is tantamount to saying, "Yes, you have said who I am." Jesus claims for Himself the title "Son of man." Dr. Warfield said that this is the highest title the Lord had. This is a title the prophets used (see Daniel and Ezekiel). It was an epithet of deity. He could have claimed no greater position than to have said He was "the Son of man sitting on the right hand of power, and coming in the clouds of heaven."

> **Then the high priest rent his clothes, saying, He hath spoken blasphemy; what further need have we of witnesses? behold, now ye have heard his blasphemy [Matt. 26:65].**

"Then the high priest rent his clothes"—that is, he tears his robes, signifying extreme grief at hearing blasphemy. They think that they have a charge against Jesus now.

> **What think ye? They answered and said, He is guilty of death.**

> Then did they spit in his face, and buffeted him; and others smote him with the palms of their hands,
>
> Saying, Prophesy unto us, thou Christ, Who is he that smote thee? [Matt. 26:66–68].

How they hated the Lord Jesus! This is the natural antagonism of the human heart to His goodness, His righteousness, His holiness, and the fact that He is God. Do you realize, my friend, that if you and I had only our old natures, we would try to knock God off His throne? A few years ago a crowd was saying that God was dead! Do you know why they said that? Because they would like to get Him off His throne. Human nature hates Him.

Here in the Sanhedrin He was slapped, spit upon, beaten with fists, and ridiculed.

"Saying, Prophesy unto us, thou Christ, Who is he that smote thee?" They played a game with Him. They apparently blindfolded Him, then hit Him on the face, and He was to guess who did it. They would never have let Him guess right, of course.

PETER'S DENIAL OF JESUS

We will look at this in more detail in the other Gospel records.

> Now Peter sat without in the palace: and a damsel came unto him, saying, Thou also wast with Jesus of Galilee.
>
> But he denied before them all, saying, I know not what thou sayest.
>
> And when he was gone out into the porch, another maid saw him, and said unto them that were there, This fellow was also with Jesus of Nazareth.
>
> And again he denied with an oath, I do not know the man.

> **And after a while came unto him they that stood by, and said to Peter, Surely thou also art one of them; for thy speech bewrayeth thee [Matt. 26:69–73].**

Galilean pronunciations were a little different from those used in Judea. Peter had a Galilean accent!

> **Then began he to curse and to swear, saying, I know not the man. And immediately the cock crew [Matt. 26:74].**

The poor man did not realize how weak he really was! But our Lord had prayed that his faith would not fail, and it did not.

> **And Peter remembered the word of Jesus, which said unto him, Before the cock crow, thou shalt deny me thrice. And he went out, and wept bitterly [Matt. 26:75].**

Simon Peter was in the wrong place. For him, it was the place of temptation. No alibi can be offered for his base denial. He was guilty of a heinous act. However, Peter did repent and come back into fellowship with the Lord he loved. In fact, Peter was the one to whom He gave the privilege of preaching the first sermon after the coming of the Holy Spirit at Pentecost, and *three thousand* people were saved!

CHAPTER 27

THEME: *Events surrounding the crucifixion of Jesus;
Sanhedrin delivers Jesus to Pilate; repentance of
Judas; trial before Pilate; release of Barabbas; crucifixion, death, and burial of Jesus; the tomb sealed
and a watch set*

We have come to the central fact of the gospel message: the crucifixion of Christ. When Paul defined the gospel to the Corinthians, he said, "For I delivered unto you first of all that which I also
received, how that Christ *died* for our sins according to the scriptures" (1 Cor. 15:3, italics mine). We have now come to the record of
that tremendous event.

We will see that Matthew does not give a record of the actual crucifixion. In fact, no Gospel writer does that. They merely tell what went
on around the Cross. I know that there are men who depict in graphic
terms how the nails were driven into the quivering flesh and how the
blood spurted out, but that is not in the Bible. In the inspired record it
is as if God placed the mantle of darkness over the last three hours of
the life of Jesus on the Cross and said, "This is something you cannot
look at. It is beyond human comprehension. The suffering cannot be
fathomed." It was a transaction between the Father in heaven and the
Son on the Cross. The Cross became an altar upon which the Lamb of
God, who takes away the sin of the world, was offered.

The simple statement of Matthew is, "And they crucified him."

This chapter begins with the morning after Jesus had been arrested
in the Garden of Gethsemane, after He had been brought before
Caiaphas and the Sanhedrin, after false witnesses had testified
against Him, after He had been beaten and ridiculed, and after Peter
had denied Him.

THE SANHEDRIN DELIVERS JESUS TO PILATE

When the morning was come, all the chief priests and elders of the people took counsel against Jesus to put him to death [Matt. 27:1].

They have formulated a charge against Jesus and will take Him now to the supreme court. They think they have a case which will stand up before the Roman court.

And when they had bound him, they led him away, and delivered him to Pontius Pilate the governor [Matt. 27:2].

Pilate had a palace in Jerusalem, although his headquarters were in Caesarea on the Mediterranean Sea. He was in Jerusalem at the Passover season because the city was crowded with Jews who had come to the feast, and generally there were riots on such occasions.

Then Judas, which had betrayed him, when he saw that he was condemned, repented himself, and brought again the thirty pieces of silver to the chief priests and elders [Matt. 27:3].

You see, the Lord Jesus was there when Judas came. As the chief priests and elders were leading Him through that hall to take Him to Pilate, here comes Judas. Why doesn't Judas turn to the Lord Jesus and ask forgiveness? Instead of doing that, he addressed the religious rulers—

Saying, I have sinned in that I have betrayed the innocent blood. And they said, What is that to us? see thou to that [Matt. 27:4].

In other words, "You did the job, and it's over with. We have the One we were after. We have paid you off, and we have no need of you any further."

> And he cast down the pieces of silver in the temple, and
> departed, and went and hanged himself [Matt. 27:5].

This man leaves the temple area, goes out, and hangs himself. He
could have turned to the Lord Jesus and would have been forgiven!

> And the chief priests took the silver pieces, and said, It
> is not lawful for to put them into the treasury, because it
> is the price of blood [Matt. 27:6].

How pious they are! They can't put it in the temple treasury because it
is blood money.

> And they took counsel, and bought with them the pot-
> ter's field, to bury strangers in.
>
> Wherefore that field was called, The field of blood, unto
> this day [Matt. 27:7–8].

This was a remarkable fulfillment of prophecy—

> Then was fulfilled that which was spoken by Jeremy the
> prophet, saying, And they took the thirty pieces of sil-
> ver, the price of him that was valued, whom they of the
> children of Israel did value;
>
> And gave them for the potter's field, as the Lord ap-
> pointed me [Matt. 27:9–10].

You will find this prophecy alluded to in Jeremiah 18:1–4 and evidently quoted from Zechariah 11:12–13. It is credited to Jeremiah
simply because in Jesus' day Jeremiah was the first of the books of the
prophets, and that section was identified by the name of the first book.
    The significant thing is that Jesus was present when Judas re-
turned with his thirty pieces of silver. In fact, Jesus was on His way to
die—even for Judas. Our Lord had given him an opportunity to come
back to Him there in the Garden of Gethsemane, and He had said,

"Friend, wherefore art thou come?" And even at this eleventh hour, Judas could have turned to the Lord Jesus and would have been forgiven.

PILATE QUESTIONS JESUS

And Jesus stood before the governor: and the governor asked him, saying, Art thou the King of the Jews? And Jesus said unto him, Thou sayest [Matt. 27:11].

You see, the religious rulers wanted to get rid of Jesus because of what they considered blasphemy. You remember that when the high priest put Him on oath and asked Him if He was the Christ, the Son of God, Jesus said that He was. And further He said, "Hereafter shall ye see the Son of man sitting on the right hand of power, and coming in the clouds of heaven" (Matt. 26:64). To the religious rulers that was blasphemy, and they would have stoned Him on that charge, but Rome did not allow the Jews to carry out the death penalty. So they had to deliver Jesus to Pilate with a charge that would stick in a Roman court. Treason would be one that would stick, and so Jesus was charged with claiming to be the King of the Jews.

The answer of Jesus to the charge was, "Thou sayest"—or, "It is as you say."

And when he was accused of the chief priests and elders, he answered nothing [Matt. 27:12].

They made certain false charges against Him, and our Lord didn't bother to answer them.

Then said Pilate unto him, Hearest thou not how many things they witness against thee?

And he answered him to never a word; insomuch that the governor marvelled greatly [Matt. 27:13–14].

He was the Lamb of God, you see, who before the shearers was dumb (see Isa. 53:7).

> Now at that feast the governor was wont to release unto the people a prisoner, whom they would.
>
> And they had then a notable prisoner, called Barabbas [Matt. 27:15–16].

Matthew does not give us the byplay that took place. All the other Gospel writers add a great deal to this account, but Matthew simply states the bare facts.

Obviously, Pilate felt that the religious rulers had no basis for requesting the death penalty. Jesus had not incited rebellion against Rome. Others had, but Jesus had not. Pilate had a problem on his hands. He wanted to please the religious leaders in order to maintain peace in Jerusalem, but he felt that he could not arbitrarily sentence the Lord Jesus to death. So he hit upon a solution to the problem. Since it was his habit to release a Jewish prisoner during the Passover celebration, he would offer the crowd a choice: Jesus; or a very notorious prisoner called Barabbas, who was guilty of murder, robbery, treason—the whole bit.

> Therefore when they were gathered together, Pilate said unto them, Whom will ye that I release unto you? Barabbas, or Jesus which is called Christ? [Matt. 27:17].

Pilate thought that the crowd would certainly ask that Jesus be released—the contrast between Him and Barabbas was so evident.

> For he knew that for envy they had delivered him [Matt. 27:18].

Pilate was a clever politician. He could see what was taking place, and he was sure that the crowd would ask for Barabbas to be crucified and Jesus to be released. This would give him a happy "out" to this situation.

> When he was set down on the judgment seat, his wife sent unto him, saying, Have thou nothing to do with that

> just man: for I have suffered many things this day in a
> dream because of him [Matt. 27:19].

Pilate's wife was as superstitious as could be. Perhaps she was tied up in a mystery religion, and this sort of thing could have been satanic. I do not believe that this warning came from God. If she had been a just woman, she would have investigated Jesus and found out more about Him. She did not, however. She was simply superstitious and asked her husband to have nothing to do with Him.

> But the chief priests and elders persuaded the multitude
> that they should ask Barabbas, and destroy Jesus [Matt.
> 27:20].

You see, the religious rulers were clever politicians themselves. They circulated among the crowd saying, "Ask that Barabbas be delivered and Jesus be destroyed."

> The governor answered and said unto them, Whether of
> the twain will ye that I release unto you? They said,
> Barabbas [Matt. 27:21].

Pilate was taken aback. He had not known how low religion would stoop.

> Pilate saith unto them, What shall I do then with Jesus
> which is called Christ? They all say unto him, Let him
> be crucified [Matt. 27:22].

Imagine a Roman judge asking a crowd what he should do with a prisoner! Pilate was the judge, and he should make the decision. The Gospel of John tells us that Pilate repeatedly called Jesus inside the judgment hall and questioned Him privately. His thought seemed to be, "Jesus, if You will cooperate with me, I can get You out of this, and it will get me off this hot seat I'm on!" But the Lord Jesus would not defend Himself. When we analyze this mock trial, we come to the conclusion that Pilate was the one on trial and, actually, that Jesus was the Judge.

Pilate had to make a decision relative to Him; so he asked the crowd, "What shall I do then with Jesus which is called Christ?" The answer came back to him—it was flung in his face—"Let him be crucified!"

> **And the governor said, Why, what evil hath he done? But they cried out the more, saying, Let him be crucified [Matt. 27:23].**

A mob never has a reason.

> **When Pilate saw that he could prevail nothing, but that rather a tumult was made, he took water, and washed his hands before the multitude, saying, I am innocent of the blood of this just person: see ye to it [Matt. 27:24].**

Pilate called for a basin of water and washed his hands, declaring that he would have nothing to do with the execution of Jesus. But it was not that easy. He had to make a decision—every man does. It was John Newton who wrote:

> "What think ye of Christ?" is the test,
>   To try both your state and your scheme;
> You cannot be right in the rest,
>   Unless you think rightly of Him.

Although Pilate washed his hands, the bitter irony of it is that in the oldest creed of the church stand these words: " . . . crucified under Pontius Pilate." The blood of Jesus was on his hands no matter how much he washed them.

> **Then answered all the people, and said, His blood be on us, and on our children [Matt. 27:25].**

Unfortunately, that has been the case, and it can be so demonstrated.

> **Then released he Barabbas unto them: and when he had scourged Jesus, he delivered him to be crucified [Matt. 27:26].**

Pilate was willing to stoop this low himself. He had to make a decision, and his decision, of course, was one of rejection.

> **Then the soldiers of the governor took Jesus into the common hall, and gathered unto him the whole band of soldiers [Matt. 27:27].**

The soldiers were free to do with Him as they pleased. He became a plaything for this brutal, cruel crowd.

> **And they stripped him, and put on him a scarlet robe.**

> **And when they had platted a crown of thorns, they put it upon his head, and a reed in his right hand: and they bowed the knee before him, and mocked him, saying, Hail, King of the Jews! [Matt. 27:28–29].**

It is frightful what they did to Him—

> **And they spit upon him, and took the reed, and smote him on the head [Matt. 27:30].**

The soldiers took this opportunity to have their fun with Him before He was crucified. Since He was going to die anyway, they could mutilate Him and do anything they wished with Him. They played a cruel Roman game known as "hot-hand" with their prisoners. All the soldiers would show the prisoner their fists. Then they would blindfold the prisoner, and all but one would hit him as hard as they could. Then they would remove the blindfold, and if the prisoner was still conscious, he was to guess which soldier did not hit him. Obviously, the prisoner could never guess the right one. They would continue this until they had beaten the prisoner to a pulp. I believe that the Lord Jesus was so mutilated that you would not have recognized Him. "As many were astonied at thee; his visage was so marred more than any man, and his form more than the sons of men" (Isa. 52:14).

> **And after that they had mocked him, they took the robe off from him, and put his own raiment on him, and led him away to crucify him.**

> **And as they came out, they found a man of Cyrene, Simon by name: him they compelled to bear his cross [Matt. 27:31–32].**

Jesus was subjected to abject humiliation and untold suffering. We are given the impression here that He was too weak to carry His cross because of the ordeal to which the soldiers had subjected Him.

THE CRUCIFIXION

> **And when they were come unto a place called Golgotha, that is to say, a place of a skull [Matt. 27:33].**

That place can be identified, I believe, as Gordon's Calvary (named for General Gordon who selected it as the probable site of Golgotha). I have looked around that area. After all these years and the things that have happened to the city Jerusalem, it is difficult to make a judgment, but certainly the topography of Gordon's choice is close to the biblical description of Golgotha. It is a place that resembles a skull.

> **They gave him vinegar to drink mingled with gall: and when he had tasted thereof, he would not drink [Matt. 27:34].**

This is a fulfillment of Psalm 69:21: "They gave me also gall for my meat; and in my thirst they gave me vinegar to drink."

> **And they crucified him, and parted his garments, casting lots: that it might be fulfilled which was spoken by the prophet, They parted my garments among them, and upon my vesture did they cast lots [Matt. 27:35].**

The prophecy is from Psalm 22, which presents a graphic picture of death by crucifixion: "They part my garments among them and cast lots upon my vesture" (Ps. 22:18).

> **And sitting down they watched him there [Matt. 27:36].**

In my opinion it is here that we see humanity which has reached its lowest depth. You don't need to go to skid row or to a prison to see man at his lowest, you can see him here—"sitting down they watched him there." I believe that in this crowd was Saul of Tarsus. Later on when he wrote to Timothy, he called himself the chief of sinners (see 1 Tim. 1:15), and I believe he called himself that because he *was* the chief of sinners.

> **And set up over his head his accusation written, THIS IS JESUS THE KING OF THE JEWS.**
>
> **Then were there two thieves crucified with him, one on the right hand, and another on the left.**
>
> **And they that passed by reviled him, wagging their heads,**
>
> **And saying, Thou that destroyest the temple, and buildest it in three days, save thyself. If thou be the Son of God, come down from the cross [Matt. 27:37–40].**

"If thou be the Son of God, come down from the cross." Notice that they raise the doubt—"*If* thou be the Son of God . . ." Little did they know that since He is the Son of God, He will not come down from the Cross. He doesn't have to prove anything at this point. He is now dying for the sins of the world.

Likewise also the chief priests mocking him, with the scribes and elders, said [Matt. 27:41].

You would think that after this pack of bloodhounds had succeeded in getting Him on the Cross, they would go home and let Him die in peace, but they didn't. They stayed there taunting Him while there was still life in His body.

He saved others; himself he cannot save. If he be the King of Israel, let him now come down from the cross, and we will believe him [Matt. 27:42].

That is a true statement—"He saved others; himself he cannot save." If He were to save you and me, He would have had to die on that cross. If He had come down from the Cross, you and I would have to be executed for our sins. We deserve it; we are hell-doomed sinners. Christ was taking our place there. As surely as He took the place of Barabbas, He took our place.

"Let him now come down from the cross, and we will believe him." Would they have believed Him? I don't think so.

He trusted in God; let him deliver him now, if he will have him: for he said, I am the Son of God [Matt. 27:43].

You can see that the crowd understood that Jesus claimed deity.

The thieves also, which were crucified with him, cast the same in his teeth [Matt. 27:44].

Matthew calls our attention to the thieves who were crucified with Him and the fact that they joined with the religious rulers in mocking Him. He does *not* call our attention to the fact that one of the thieves finally turned to Jesus. The Kingdom presented in Matthew will be on this earth, and the thief who repented went with Christ to paradise that very day.

Now from the sixth hour there was darkness over all the land unto the ninth hour [Matt. 27:45].

Our Lord was put on the Cross at the third hour, which would be nine o'clock in the morning. By twelve noon, man had done all he could to the Son of God. Then at the noon hour, darkness settled down, and that cross became an altar on which the Lamb who taketh away the sin of the world was offered.

And about the ninth hour Jesus cried with a loud voice, saying, Eli, Eli, lama sabachthani? that is to say, My God, my God, why hast thou forsaken me? [Matt. 27:46].

We find the answer to that question in Psalm 22. It opens with these words: "My God, my God, why hast thou forsaken me? why art thou so far from helping me, and from the words of my roaring?" Then we read the answer in verse 3: *"But thou art holy . . ."* (Ps. 22:1, 3, italics mine). When my sin is put upon Jesus, God has to withdraw. Our Savior had to be executed if He were going to take my sin and yours.

Some of them that stood there, when they heard that, said, This man calleth for Elias.

And straightway one of them ran, and took a sponge, and filled it with vinegar, and put it on a reed, and gave him to drink [Matt. 27:47–48].

Why? To fulfill prophecy—"They gave me also gall for my meat; and in my thirst they gave me vinegar to drink" (Ps. 69:21).

The rest said, Let be, let us see whether Elias will come to save him.

Jesus, when he had cried again with a loud voice, yielded up the ghost [Matt. 27:49–50].

Notice how He died: He "yielded up the ghost"—that is, He dismissed His spirit. As a pastor I have often heard the death rattle, the gasp for that last breath which we all want so badly. Our Lord didn't go that way. He dismissed His spirit. He went willingly.

INCIDENTS CONNECTED WITH HIS DEATH

At the death of Christ several very notable things took place. One was an earthquake. Another was that the veil in the temple, the curtain which separated the Holy of Holies from the rest of the temple, was torn in two—

> **And, behold, the veil of the temple was rent in twain from the top to the bottom; and the earth did quake, and the rocks rent [Matt. 27:51].**

Notice that the veil was torn, not from the bottom to the top but from top to bottom. It was rent by God, not by man. The veil symbolizes the body of Jesus. When His body was rent upon the Cross—when He had paid the penalty for your sin and my sin in His own body—then the way was opened into the presence of God. Therefore, you and I don't have to have a priest or a preacher go into the presence of God for us; we can go directly to the throne of God *through Christ.* Let's emphasize that the *only* way to the Father is through His Son. "For there is one God, and one mediator between God and men, the man Christ Jesus" (1 Tim. 2:5).

> **And the graves were opened; and many bodies of the saints which slept arose,**
>
> **And came out of the graves after his resurrection, and went into the holy city, and appeared unto many [Matt. 27:52–53].**

This is an event that is mentioned only by Matthew. We wish more had been told. I can only say that I believe it happened just the way Matthew tells it and that those who arose were part of that great company who went to heaven when Christ led captivity captive at His ascension (see Eph. 4:8–10). The earthquake mentioned in verse 51 was an intelligent quake, not haphazard, because the graves were opened by it, and "many bodies of the saints which slept arose"—just certain ones.

"And [they] appeared unto many." There were many witnesses who saw these certain folk because, according to Matthew, they "went into the holy city and appeared unto many." There is a very excellent treatment of this, and the other miracles which occurred at this time, in a little booklet entitled *The Six Miracles of Calvary*, written by Bishop Nicholson. If you are interested in pursuing this study, I recommend it to you. It is a rich little book.

> **Now when the centurion, and they that were with him, watching Jesus, saw the earthquake, and those things that were done, they feared greatly, saying, Truly this was the Son of God [Matt. 27:54].**

In Mark's account it says this: "And when the centurion, which stood over against him, saw that he so cried out, and gave up the ghost, he said, Truly this man was the Son of God" (Mark 15:39). Apparently, that Roman centurion, who was in charge of the actual crucifixion, stood beneath Christ's cross. As he witnessed some of the miraculous events during this time and as he saw the Lord Jesus dismiss His spirit, the fact was confirmed to him that this was the Son of God. I believe that the centurion became a saved man. He probably did not know a great deal; he had never read Strong's theology or Hodges' theology, nor Augustine's *City of God*, nor any of my books, but he knew enough to take his place beneath the Cross of Christ. And that is all that God asks of any sinner.

> **And many women were there beholding afar off, which followed Jesus from Galilee, ministering unto him:**
>
> **Among which was Mary Magdalene, and Mary the mother of James and Joses, and the mother of Zebedee's children [Matt. 27:55–56].**

JESUS BURIED IN JOSEPH'S TOMB

When the even was come, there came a rich man of Arimathaea, named Joseph, who also himself was Jesus' disciple [Matt. 27:57].

We did not know that he was a disciple until this event. It is interesting to see that the very thing which caused the apostles to scatter seems to have drawn into the open others who, up to this time, would have been called secret disciples. Joseph of the town of Arimathaea stepped out and declared his faith.

He went to Pilate, and begged the body of Jesus. Then Pilate commanded the body to be delivered [Matt. 27:58].

Joseph went to Pilate on the basis that he was a disciple of Jesus.

And when Joseph had taken the body, he wrapped it in a clean linen cloth [Matt. 27:59].

John tells us that Nicodemus worked with Joseph in preparing the body of Jesus for burial—"And there came also Nicodemus, which at the first came to Jesus by night, and brought a mixture of myrrh and aloes, about an hundred pound weight. Then took they the body of Jesus, and wound it in linen clothes with the spices, as the manner of the Jews is to bury" (John 19:39–40). These two men, who apparently had been in the background, now came out in the open as the disciples of Jesus. It is interesting to note that only loving hands touched the body of Jesus after His death.

And laid it in his own new tomb, which he had hewn out in the rock: and he rolled a great stone to the door of the sepulchre, and departed.

And there was Mary Magdalene, and the other Mary, sitting over against the sepulchre [Matt. 27:60–61].

Note this one tender incident in connection with the death of Jesus. Several women were faithful and stayed at the cross. They were loyal when the apostles had fled.

Near the hill, which we designate as Gordon's Calvary, is a tomb which is pointed out as the tomb in which Jesus was buried. It is called the Garden Tomb. We have no way of knowing if this was the tomb of Jesus; frankly, I have my doubts. There are many sepulchres in that area, and it could have been any one of them. I feel sure that His tomb is in that area, and the Garden Tomb is as good a choice as any of them. But to determine the exact location of Golgotha and of the tomb and to make them sacred shrines is not Christ's intention. I saw a woman go into the tomb and on hands and knees kiss the floor where the bodies were placed! That has no value. What our Lord wants us to do is to believe the gospel—that He died for our sins, was buried, and rose again—and to take that good news to the whole world.

THE SEPULCHRE IS SEALED AND THE WATCH SET

Now the next day, that followed the day of the preparation, the chief priests and Pharisees came together unto Pilate,

Saying, Sir, we remember that that deceiver said, while he was yet alive, after three days I will rise again.

Command therefore that the sepulchre be made sure until the third day, lest his disciples come by night, and steal him away, and say unto the people, He is risen from the dead: so the last error shall be worse than the first.

Pilate said unto them, Ye have a watch: go your way, make it as sure as ye can.

So they went, and made the sepulchre sure, sealing the stone, and setting a watch [Matt. 27:62–66]

The zeal of the enemy actually gives a confirmation of Jesus' resurrection! If they had gone off and left that tomb as it was, their later explanation for the tomb's being empty might be plausible. But, my friend, when you've got a tomb that is sealed and a Roman guard around it watching it, their claim that the apostles stole away the body of Jesus sounds pretty silly. The enemies of Jesus went to a lot of trouble to make the sepulchre sure, and that fact furnishes a marvelous confirmation of His resurrection.

Another interesting point is that when our Lord had told His disciples that He would rise again the third day, they had told a great many people, and the religious rulers got word of it. As soon as they could get another audience with Pilate, they said, "Look, Jesus made the statement that He would rise again the third day, and we want to make sure His body stays in that tomb." Of course, they did not believe He would be resurrected, but neither did the apostles believe that He would come out of that tomb alive

CHAPTER 28

THEME: The resurrection of Jesus; the giving of the Great Commission

The arch of the gospel rests upon two great pillars: (1) the death of Christ, and (2) the resurrection of Christ. Listen to the apostle Paul as he defines the gospel: "For I delivered unto you first of all that which I also received, how that Christ died for our sins according to the scriptures; And that he was buried, and that he rose again the third day according to the scriptures" (1 Cor. 15:3–4).

In the previous chapter we have seen the death and burial of the Lord Jesus, and in this chapter we will see His resurrection. Both are essential to my salvation and yours. "Who [Jesus] was delivered for our offences, and was raised again for our justification" (Rom. 4:25). He was made sin for us that we might be made the righteousness of God in Him.

The unique fact of the gospel is the Resurrection. All other religions record the death of their leader. Only the Christian faith records the Resurrection of its Founder. All other religious leaders are dead. *Only Jesus is alive.* This is important and imperative to know.

No Gospel writer gives the complete details which concern the Resurrection. Each records that aspect of the Resurrection which contributes to the furtherance of the purpose which the Spirit had in mind. Therefore the four Gospels present a composite picture. No writer is seeing to give the entire and complete record but only that which serves his purpose. All the Gospel accounts need to be put together to get the total picture, and no conflict or contradiction will appear among them.

Regarding the order of events connected with the resurrection of Christ, I would like to share with you a very fine note found in *The Scofield Reference Bible* on page 1043:

> The order of events, combining the four narratives, is as follows: Three women, Mary Magdalene, and Mary the mother

of James, and Salome, start for the sepulchre, followed by
other women bearing spices. The three find the stone rolled
away, and Mary Magdalene goes to tell the disciples (Lk.
23:55—24:9; John 20:1, 2). Mary, the mother of James and
Joses, draws nearer the tomb and sees the angel of the Lord (Mt.
28:2). She goes back to meet the other women following with
the spices. Meanwhile Peter and John, warned by Mary Magdalene, arrive, look in, and go away (John 20:3-10). Mary Magdalene returns weeping, sees the two angels and then Jesus (John
20:11-18), and goes as He bade her to tell the disciples. Mary
(mother of James and Joses), meanwhile, has met the women
with the spices and, returning with them, they see the two
angels (Lk. 24:4, 5; Mk. 16:5). They also receive the angelic
message, and, going to seek the disciples, are met by Jesus (Mt.
28:8-10).

The order of our Lord's appearances would seem to be: On
the day of His resurrection: (1) To Mary Magdalene (John
20:14-18). (2) To the women returning from the tomb with the
angelic message (Mt. 28:8-10). (3) To Peter, probably in the
afternoon (Lk. 24:34; 1 Cor. 15:5). (4) To the Emmaus disciples
toward evening (Lk. 24:13-31). (5) To the apostles, except
Thomas (Lk. 24:36-43; John 20:19-24). Eight days afterward:
(1) To the apostles, Thomas being present (John 20:24-29). In
Galilee: (1) To the seven by the Lake of Tiberias (John 21:1-23).
(2) On a mountain, to the apostles and five hundred brethren
(1 Cor. 15:6). At Jerusalem and Bethany again: (1) To James
(1 Cor. 15:7). (2) To the eleven (Mt. 28:16-20; Mk. 16:14-20;
Lk. 24:33-53; Acts 1:3-12). To Paul: (1) Near Damascus (Acts
9:3-6; 1 Cor. 15:8). (2) In the temple (Acts 22:17-21; 23:11). To
Stephen, outside Jerusalem (Acts 7:55). To John on Patmos
(Rev. 1:10-19).

Matthew presents Jesus as the King. The features of the resurrection
story which contain the element of the spectacular and sensational are
given. There is a fanfare of trumpets in the account given in Matthew.
He was born a King. He lived as a King. He died a King, and He rose

from the dead a King. Matthew tells of the earthquake, of the angel's descent, of the stone rolled away, of the frightened guards, and of the effort by the religious rulers to cover up the fact of the empty tomb.

Compare Luke's Gospel with Matthew's account. There is quietness and a subdued tone which characterizes Luke's purpose. The women come in the stillness of the early morning, and the stone is already rolled away. The Lord Jesus appears to two unknown disciples on an obscure road leading to Emmaus and then to the disciples in a secret room of a house of unknown address. Luke is recording the human story while Matthew is presenting Him in His kingly office. Both records are accurate, as are the records in the other two Gospels, but they are presented from four different viewpoints.

APPROACH OF THE TWO MARYS TO THE TOMB

In the end of the sabbath, as it began to dawn toward the first day of the week, came Mary Magdalene and the other Mary to see the sepulchre [Matt. 28:1].

The other Gospel records tell us that they were bringing sweet spices to anoint the body of Jesus. It is difficult to identify the "other Mary." Tradition states that she was the mother of James and Joses.

And, behold, there was a great earthquake: for the angel of the Lord descended from heaven, and came and rolled back the stone from the door, and sat upon it [Matt. 28:2].

Why was it necessary to roll back the stone? To let Jesus out? No, He was gone when the stone was rolled back. The tomb was not opened to let Him out but to let *them* in.

His countenance was like lightning, and his raiment white as snow [Matt 28:3].

It is interesting to note the description of the angel because this is very unusual in Scripture (see Dan. 10:6; Rev. 10:1 for other descriptions).

> **And for fear of him the keepers did shake, and became as dead men [Matt. 28:4].**

I can imagine that the guards were very happy to leave after this episode! They were helpless in the presence of the angel.

> **And the angel answered and said unto the women, Fear not ye: for I know that ye seek Jesus, which was crucified [Matt. 28:5].**

"Fear not"—when the supernatural touches the natural, it is always with a word to allay fear.

> **He is not here: for he is risen, as he said. Come, see the place where the Lord lay [Matt. 28:6].**

This is the divine announcement of the Resurrection. Jesus had left the tomb before the stone had been rolled away. Later He would enter a room with a locked door. The glorified body of Jesus was radically different from the body with which He was born.

> **And go quickly, and tell his disciples that he is risen from the dead; and, behold, he goeth before you into Galilee; there shall ye see him: lo, I have told you [Matt. 28:7].**

The angelic announcement ceased at this point. From here on the message would be told by human lips—"Come, see. . . . go quickly, and tell." But before any individual attempts to witness, he must first have an unshakable conviction of the truth of the Resurrection. He must have it settled in his own mind that Christ died for his sins and was buried—"Come, see the place where the Lord lay"—and that

Christ rose again—"He is not here: for he is risen." Then with these convictions, he can "go quickly, and tell." My friend, you and I are to *go* and we are to *tell*.

APPEARANCE OF JESUS TO THE TWO MARYS

And they departed quickly from the sepulchre with fear and great joy; and did run to bring his disciples word [Matt. 28:8].

Note the mingled feelings of the women—fear and great joy.

And as they went to tell his disciples, behold, Jesus met them, saying, All hail. And they came and held him by the feet, and worshipped him [Matt. 28:9].

This seems to contradict the encounter of Mary Magdalene with her resurrected Lord. In John 20:17 we find this: "Jesus saith unto her, Touch me not; for I am not yet ascended to my Father: but go to my brethren, and say unto them, I ascend unto my Father, and your Father, and to my God, and your God." The explanation is that between these two encounters Jesus had ascended to His Father and had presented His precious blood in heaven's Holy of Holies.

Then said Jesus unto them, Be not afraid: go tell my brethren that they go into Galilee, and there shall they see me [Matt. 28:10].

He made an appointment to see them in Galilee.

ALIBI OF THE KEEPERS

Now when they were going, behold, some of the watch came into the city, and shewed unto the chief priests all the things that were done [Matt. 28:11].

These soldiers who were on guard duty went into the city and reported to the chief priests. They didn't know when Jesus left the tomb. All they knew was that after the stone was rolled away, they took a look inside the tomb, and the body wasn't there! The entire episode had nearly frightened them to death. They could have been executed for allowing the body of Jesus to disappear under their very eyes.

> **And when they were assembled with the elders, and had taken counsel, they gave large money unto the soldiers,**
>
> **Saying, Say ye, His disciples came by night, and stole him away while we slept [Matt. 28:12–13].**

This is not a very plausible explanation! Imagine a soldier, especially a Roman soldier, assigned guard duty in a certain place and given strict orders to stand guard over a certain thing and to prohibit all trespassing. Suppose someone did come and take away the thing he was assigned to guard. And suppose that his explanation to his commanding officer was, "I went to sleep." What do you think would happen to him?

> **And if this come to the governor's ears, we will persuade him, and secure you [Matt. 28:14].**

In others words, "Don't worry if this reaches the ears of the governor. We won't let him put you before a firing squad."

> **So they took the money, and did as they were taught: and this saying is commonly reported among the Jews until this day [Matt. 28:15].**

A bribe aided in persuading them to offer this feeble excuse. This was the first century alibi to explain away the resurrection of Christ. Unbelief has now had nineteen centuries to think it over, and there are other alibis. However, none yet have been offered that can explain away the documentary evidence.

THE GREAT COMMISSION

In our contemporary society we have two opposing viewpoints regarding this so-called Great Commission. Frankly, I think both of them are extreme. Our Lord's commission to His disciples as recorded by Matthew is a source of controversy. One extreme group feels that the Great Commission contains the only command for the church. That is it, and they hang on to it. The other extreme group feels that it has no meaning for our day and that it should be excluded from the church program. It seems to me that both of these groups are in error.

We have endeavored to show that Matthew has direct *application* for us, and certainly the Great Commission has an application for us in our day. This does not mean that it will not find a final and full meaning in the future—I think it will. But, as it is obvious that Matthew did not give the total record of the Resurrection, neither did he give us the total commission. I feel that everything our Lord said on any subject should be put together and given as a composite in order to give a full-orbed command for the present day as well as for the future. The commission in Matthew should be considered with the commission recorded in the other gospel records and especially with Acts 1:8: "But ye shall receive power, after that the Holy Ghost is come upon you: and ye shall be witnesses unto me both in Jerusalem, and in all Judaea, and in Samaria, and unto the uttermost part of the earth." We are to be His witnesses, and we are to be endued with power from on high.

> **Then the eleven disciples went away into Galilee, into a mountain where Jesus had appointed them.**
>
> **And when they saw him, they worshipped him: but some doubted [Matt. 28:16–17].**

Some worshiped and some doubted—that is how it has been for over nineteen hundred years! And, my friend, you are in one category or the other.

And Jesus came and spake unto them, saying, All power is given unto me in heaven and in earth [Matt. 28:18].

He was speaking as the King.

Go ye therefore, and teach all nations, baptizing them in the name of the Father, and of the Son, and of the Holy Ghost [Matt. 28:19].

This, I am confident, will have a real application during the Great Tribulation period and even during the Millennium. But, my friend, it has an application for us today, also.

"Baptizing them in the name of the Father, and of the Son, and of the Holy Ghost [Spirit]." Baptism by water in the name of the Trinity has been practiced by the church from its beginning. Even Paul, who was not sent to baptize (see 1 Cor. 1:14–17), practiced this rite of the early church. "The name of the Father, and of the Son, and of the Holy Ghost [Spirit]" is evidence for the Trinity of the Godhead.

Teaching them to observe all things whatsoever I have commanded you: and, lo, I am with you alway, even unto the end of the world. Amen [Matt. 28:20].

Notice that teaching is part of the work of the church (see Eph. 4:11). The teachings of Jesus are found not only in the Gospels but in the Epistles (see 1 Thess. 4:2).

"Lo, I am with you alway even unto the end of the world." The word *world* is the Greek *aiōn*, meaning age. Our Lord promises to be with us right on through to the very end of the age. In His *power* the Great Commission can be carried out.

We have looked at the Great Commission, now let's consider the great omission. Do you see what Matthew has omitted from his record? There is no *ascension* of Christ here. Why? The obvious reason is that the Kingdom will be here upon this earth, and Matthew leaves the King here on earth because this is where the King is to be. Luke 24:49–53 and Acts 1:6–11 record the ascension of Christ. At the time of the rapture of the church, the Lord Jesus will take His own out of the world to be with Himself, and the Ascension is essential for that event.

However, Matthew is the Gospel of the King. Jesus was born a King. He lived as a King. He died as a King. He rose again as a King. And, my friend, He will be coming again to this earth as King of kings and Lord of lords! I hope you will bow to Him today.

BIBLIOGRAPHY
(Recommended for Further Study)

Frank, Harry Thomas, editor. *Hammond's Atlas of the Bible Lands.* Maplewood, New Jersey: Hammond Inc., 1977. (Excellent and inexpensive.)

Gaebelein, Arno C. *The Gospel of Matthew.* Neptune, New Jersey Loizeaux Brothers, Inc., 1910.

Ironside, H. A. *Expository Notes on the Gospel of Matthew.* Neptune, New Jersey: Loizeaux Brothers, Inc., n.d. (Especially good for young Christians.)

Kelley, William. *Lectures on the Gospel of Matthew.* Neptune, New Jersey: Loizeaux Brothers, Inc., 1868.

McGee, J. Vernon. *Moving Thru Matthew.* Pasadena, California: Thru the Bible Books, 1955. (An outline study.)

Pentecost, J. Dwight. *The Parables of Our Lord.* Grand Rapids, Michigan: Zondervan Publishing House, 1982.

Pentecost, J. Dwight. *The Words and Works of Jesus Christ.* Grand Rapids, Michigan: Zondervan Publishing House, 1981.

Scroggie, W. Graham. *A Guide to the Gospels.* London: Pickering & Inglis, 1948. (Excellent for personal or group study.)

Thomas, W. H. Griffith. *Outline Studies in Matthew.* Grand Rapids, Michigan: Eerdmans, 1961.

Toussaint, Stanley D. *Matthew: Behold the King.* Portland, Oregon: Multnomah Press, 1980.

Vos, Howard F. *Beginnings in the Life of Christ.* Chicago, Illinois: Moody Press, 1975.

Vos, Howard F. *Matthew: A Study Guide Commentary*. Grand Rapids, Michigan: Zondervan Publishing House, 1979.

Walvoord, John F. *Gospel of Matthew*. Chicago, Illinois: Moody Press, 1975.